LANSDOWNE PUBLIC LIBRARY

LOVE
AND
MARRIAGE

A Guide for Young People

LOVE AND MARRIAGE

A Guide for Young People

By Curtis E. Avery

and Theodore B. Johannis, Jr.

HARCOURT BRACE JOVANOVICH, INC.   New York

Curriculum-Related Books are relevant to current interests of young people and to topics in the school curriculum.

The authors are grateful to the following for permission to reprint copyrighted materials:

Abingdon Press (from *Success in Marriage*, by David R. Mace); Associated Press Newsfeatures (article by Mary Feeley, May 1, 1967); *Changing Times* ("Some Things the Ladies Told Us," copyright 1965 by the Kiplinger Washington Editors, Inc.); Holt, Rinehart & Winston, Inc., and Jonathan Cape Ltd. (from "Take Something Like a Star" from *The Poetry of Robert Frost* edited by Edward Connery Lathem. Copyright 1949, © 1969 by Holt, Rinehart & Winston, Inc.); Alfred A. Knopf, Inc. (from "On Friendship," from *The Prophet*, by Kahlil Gibran. Copyright 1923 by Kahlil Gibran, copyright 1951 by Administrators C.T.A. of Kahlil Gibran Estate and Mary G. Gibran); Alfred A. Knopf, Inc., and Constable & Co., Ltd. ("On the Birth of His Son," from *Translations from the Chinese*, by Arthur Waley. Copyright 1919, 1941 by Alfred A. Knopf, Inc., copyright 1947 by Arthur Waley); McGraw-Hill Book Co. (from "Ideal Woman" and "Madness in Her Method," from *Nights with Armour*, by Richard Armour. Copyright 1958 by Richard Armour); *The Oregonian* ("Swazi Matriarchy," April 26, 1967); *Saturday Review* and Robert Varga ("Dilemmas of a Househusband," by Robert Varga. Copyright 1965 Saturday Review, Inc.).

Copyright © 1971 by Harcourt Brace Jovanovich, Inc.

All rights reserved. No part of this publication may be reproduced or transmitted in any form or by any means, electronic or mechanical, including photocopy, recording, or any information storage and retrieval system, without permission in writing from the publisher.

First Edition

ISBN 0-15-249531-2

Library of Congress Catalog Card Number: 73-151027

Printed in the United States of America

Contents

	Preface	1
1	Your Ideas about Marriage	5
2	The Social Science View of Marriage	15
3	Sex Roles	25
4	The Marriage Team	41
5	Marriage Income	51
6	Money	65
7	Leisure Time	81
8	Family and Family Roles	93
9	Neighbors and Friends	111
10	Love	123
11	Sex and Marriage	135
12	Planning for Parenthood	149
13	Values	163
	Sources	169

Preface

About 90 percent of all Americans are married at least once in their lifetimes. Quite a few marry several times, in an effort to make a successful marriage. People don't always agree on what constitutes a successful marriage, but everyone knows that a marriage is a sort of job and that it has to be worked at to make it successful by any standard. In order to learn how to go about the job of marriage, you must first find out just who you are and what your ideas about marriage may be.

Each person is different from everyone else in some ways and like other people in certain ways. Bringing these differences and likenesses into focus is the kernel of the marriage job. These differences and likenesses are influenced by education, socio-economic status, race, religion, beliefs, values, and a great many other factors. All of these factors probably control your ideas about what marriage is or can be. After you are married, you may discover that your ideas are different from those of the person you married. In that case, there may be trouble developing. Even if you both share the same essential ideas, some of them may not fit the requirements of modern marriage—or, even more importantly, the requirements of modern life in general. According to statistics, there are about forty years of marriage ahead (if you are just beginning), and there will be a lot of changes in the world and in the economy and in ideas in those forty years. But if you understand the basic concepts of marriage, and also recognize and accept the differences between your ideas about marriage and those of other people, including your husband or wife, you can make a go of it.

This book is not a cookbook-style set of directions on "how to succeed in marriage." Its purpose is to help you discover your own ideas about marriage, and adjust them if necessary in accordance with fundamental principles that probably have not changed in a thousand years or so. Essentially, marriage for you is not much different from marriage for your grandparents, great-grandparents, and the billions of other marriages proceeding those. Furthermore, this book is different from most other books on marriage. It begins where many of them leave off, and ends where some of them begin. It deals with the roots of marriage first, and with the pruning and grafting next. In this way you and the book can work together in preparation for marriage.

LOVE
AND
MARRIAGE

A Guide for Young People

1

Your Ideas about Marriage

> Hang ideas. They are tramps, vagabonds, knocking at the back door of your mind, each taking a little of your substance . . .
> —JOSEPH CONRAD: *Lord Jim*

Your ideas about marriage are your beliefs, expectations, hopes, and attitudes about the relationship between husband and wife from day to day and throughout the years. They represent your concepts of what is normal, right or wrong, desirable or not desirable in husband-wife interaction and in a couple's interaction with other people. They include, too, attitudes and convictions relating to ways of living and doing things.

It helps to have a framework, an outline, to guide you in identifying and sorting out the ideas you have now and those you will encounter. Our framework for discussion is ten categories of ideas, based on the ten areas of marriage that social scientists have found through research to be the most important. In later chapters, we shall discuss why they are important and how they influence marriage. Here the categories will simply help you organize your ideas.

1. *Sex Roles.* This term means simply the way people think, feel, and act as men or as women. In marriage, ideas about

sex roles might influence decisions about responsibility for various household chores, the way husband and wife act when they are with other people, and, of course, the way husband and wife themselves interact. The old saying "A woman's place is in the home!" is an expression of an idea about sex roles.

2. *Authority.* The area of authority concerns the way in which decisions involving the lives of both husband and wife are really made. Perhaps the wife has the final word but gives the impression of recognizing the authority of her husband, or perhaps the husband's decision is final and the wife must be submissive. Perhaps the wife is final in some aspects of daily married life, and the husband in others. Of course, authority is closely related to sex roles; but it involves more than how people behave. It involves all the ideas that husband and wife have concerning the rightful power of each marriage partner to control the actions and behavior of the other.

3. *Economics.* Everything related to money and property comes under this heading. It includes ideas about how, and by whom, the income of a married pair is obtained, and decisions on how money is spent. It also involves the question of who owns what.

4. *Use of Leisure Time.* In every marriage, there is some time when the husband and wife are not busy earning money, keeping house, fixing things, or perhaps studying. What they do with this time and how they do it are critical items in connection with all the other categories—and also in the effect on interpersonal relationships of the married couple.

5. *Family.* This area involves relationships of husband and wife with their own parents, brothers and sisters, and other relatives, and with corresponding members of the marriage partner's family. This is where the well-known "in-law problems" come into the picture.

6. *Friends.* This area involves relationships of husband and

YOUR IDEAS ABOUT MARRIAGE

wife with mutual friends and the separate relationships of each with individual friends. It includes social activity like entertaining and being entertained, and exchanging help and support with people outside the family.

7. *Love.* Marriage in America is, theoretically at least, based on love. This area, then, is concerned with what love is and how it is expressed.

8. *Sex.* Different from the category of sex roles, this area has to do with sexual relationships, including intercourse in marriage.

9. *Parenthood.* Most marriages result in children, so attitudes toward parenthood are a significant area of ideas about marriage.

10. *Values.* This area is in two parts. The first concerns the values seen in or expected from marriage itself—for instance, love, security, happiness, parenthood. Which is most important? Which least? The second part involves the values in life itself, quite apart from marriage: religion, money, success, education, personal growth, service to others, to suggest only a few. Some of these two sets of values frequently overlap.

These are the ten areas of marriage about which you have ideas. You may have some ideas that don't seem at first to fit into any of these categories, but as you go along through the book you may find that they are connected.

We are now going to sketch some reports of typical marriage situations. Use the ten areas as a guide, and try to place your ideas, and the ones expressed within these accounts, in the proper categories.

Case 1. The Kounowskys

The Kounowskys have been married five years. They have no children. Mr. Kounowsky is an automobile me-

chanic, working in a 24-hour garage. He goes to work every day just before six o'clock in the morning and he gets home in the afternoon a little after three o'clock. His wife works in a beauty parlor and goes to work about nine o'clock in the morning. Mrs. Kounowsky doesn't come home until after five o'clock, sometimes even later. When she gets home, she is usually tired and a little cross and irritable. She sometimes can't face the job of preparing supper and cleaning up afterwards; so two or three times a week the Kounowskys go out to a restaurant for their evening meal. Mr. Kounowsky complains about this, because he has to clean up and change his clothes and because of the expense involved. Mrs. Kounowsky says that after all she is earning money just as her husband is, and if she doesn't want to cook and wash dishes after a hard day at the beauty shop, she doesn't see any reason why she should. Mr. and Mrs. Kounowsky argue about this frequently, but they continue to eat out several times a week.

This is one of the most common situations in marriage today. It has implications in both the economic area and the sex role area. The ideas are really questions:

1. Is a woman's place primarily in the home and the kitchen?
2. Should the husband stay out of the kitchen regardless of anything else?
3. Does the fact that the wife also earns income that is shared by husband and wife affect the situation?
4. The situation also involves the question of authority. Who is really the boss? Or is there really a boss? Should there be a boss?

Case 2. The Clarks

The Clarks have been married only a little more than a year. Bob Clark, the husband, has a pretty good job as a

YOUR IDEAS ABOUT MARRIAGE

salesman. They have no children, and Bob makes enough money for them to live quite comfortably in a suburban area. Mrs. Clark is a very good housekeeper, and so efficient that she has a lot of spare time. She is a friendly sort and usually drops in to visit with one of her neighbors in the morning for coffee and conversation. One morning while she is talking with Mrs. Smith, she says, "You know, Bob wants to buy a new car. He thinks the one we have now is getting a little old and it doesn't give enough gas mileage. But I don't know whether I'm going to let him do it or not. We could afford it all right, I guess, but maybe we should get along with the old one for a year or so."

This is a more definite problem of authority in marriage. Also it involves left-handedly the question of sex roles. It also raises the question of how much personal family problems should be shared with neighbors and friends. Perhaps the husband should have the last say about such things as automobiles, and leave the housekeeping to his wife. On the other hand, from time immemorial many people have thought that part of a wife's duty is to make sure that her husband does not spend money foolishly—though this idea is not universal. The case, however, is a good reflector of ideas about marriage and the relationship between a married couple and the community.

Case 3. The Klines

Jim Kline is 26 years old and Carol is 22. All their friends say they have an ideal marriage and make a perfect couple. They don't have any children yet, because they want to enjoy life as much as possible while they are still young. Jim finished college and has a position in an advertising firm. In addition, he gets some income from the estate of his father, who died six years ago. They aren't wealthy; but they have a pretty good income. Carol started college but left to get married. She said that since she was marrying Jim she wouldn't have to work, and so did not need more education. Both the Klines are handsome and can afford to dress rather well. They entertain and are entertained a lot. Jim is very attentive to Carol, always doing little things for her like pulling out her chair when they sit down for dinner and holding her coat when they are going out. He helps with the housework and he likes to cook some of his own specialties. They do everything together—vacations and all their recreations involve both together. Their friends believe they never have any quarrels or disagreements. Some of the other wives in their circle sometimes tell their husbands they wish they were like Jim.

It might be in this case that the wife is somewhat swallowed up in the marriage—has less than she should have in the way of a life of her own. And it might also appear that the husband has cut himself off from male companionship to a large extent. In other words, this case might present the complete antithesis of the preceding cases. The reader can discover his own ideas by thinking about this situation very carefully.

Case 4. The Schmidts

Jake Schmidt belonged to a sort of "gang" which used to meet regularly at the corner of Second Street and Muldoon Avenue in the evenings and "just fool around." Sometimes they all went out together with their girl friends. Jake's girl was named Joan McGinnis. He was with her a great deal of the time, but he was very friendly and close to the other boys in the group. Joan got pregnant, and she and Jake were married. Jake has a job that pays him a very modest weekly salary. They found a small two-room apartment and set up housekeeping while they waited for the baby to be born. One evening Jake was passing the corner where he used to meet his friends, and one of them hailed him. He said, "Hey, Jake,

YOUR IDEAS ABOUT MARRIAGE

haven't seen you in a long time! Let's go over to Joe's and have a drink." Jake said, "I'd sure like to, but I'm married now and my old woman just wouldn't want me to. She'd drag me out by my ear if I went into a bar!" Joan is only a little more than five feet tall and Jake is more than six. She couldn't drag him out of the bar in any case, but Jake's friend accepted the explanation without question.

This case introduces a new factor in determining ideas about marriage. It has to do with the force of culture and subculture, as well as with sex roles. In some ways it also involves the question of authority in marriage. From the cultural point of view, one might say that part of the wife's job is to keep her husband "in line." Research indicates definitely that many people regard this as a primary function of marriage. However, the interpretation of ideas about marriage springing from this case is very complicated. The codes of conduct for both husband and wife before and after marriage are in conflict. The whole message seems to be that marriage changes everything. What are your ideas about this?

Case 5. The Randolphs

Don and Sue Randolph were married right after they were graduated from high school. They found a little apartment quite near Don's parents' home. Don had a job in a filling station and Sue worked part-time as a typist. She was a good typist—but a very poor cook. Don got so tired of eating out of a can that he went over to see his mother one evening and asked for help. His mother began dropping in to see Sue late in the afternoon when Sue was getting supper ready. She made suggestions about cooking, and she asked Sue to go grocery shopping with her on Saturdays.

Sue resented this. She complained to Don that his mother "was always interfering" and "ought to mind her own business." She wanted to move to another place

LOVE AND MARRIAGE

across town where it wouldn't be so easy for Don's mother to come in. But Don said he liked where they were, and he wouldn't move.

This case introduces the problem of in-laws and, again, has meaning in connection with economics and authority. The reader must sort out and arrange the specific ideas as they apply to him or her.

These situations make one realize that ideas about marriage are not easily isolated. One idea leads to another and brings up still other ideas. Each individual has a composite set of attitudes, feelings, reactions, and beliefs that underlie his individual attitudes and reactions.

The basic source of your ideas about marriage is your own personal observation and experience. You've been observing marriage, consciously or unconsciously, ever since you were born—at first probably the pattern of the marriage of your father and mother, later, perhaps, the marriage of a brother or sister. You could hardly help seeing something, at least, of the marriages of neighbors and the parents of the children you played with when you were a child. These observations gave you some ideas about marriage, whether you knew it or not. Still later, when you became more aware of marriage as a definite part of life, you consciously developed ideas about the marriages you had a chance to observe—both closely and remotely.

Among the marriages you may have observed remotely are those depicted in movies, on TV, in popular fiction, and in the "advice columns" of newspapers. How much these observations have actually influenced your ideas is debatable. A great deal depends on the ideas you had before you read or saw these materials. What you read or see may reinforce your ideas, or it may make you wish your ideas could be reconciled with the ideas expressed in fiction. But really your ideas are based chiefly on direct, personal observation.

This does not mean that your ideas are exactly the same as those you've seen reflected in the marriage of your parents or friends and acquaintances. Your reaction to all of these patterns may have been negative. You may have said to yourself, "That is not my idea of marriage." "I don't want my marriage to be like that." Even if the reaction has been negative, the basis is the same—personal observation.

The husbands and wives in the marriages you've observed, from which you developed your ideas about marriage, also have ideas about marriage, which they formed in the same way you formed yours. And the husbands and wives in the marriages *they* observed also had ideas formed in the same way. Some of what you observe may reflect ideas that people had a century ago.

Ideas about marriage in any generation reflect the needs that marriage fills for the people involved. Some of these needs are universal, and don't vary much with time and place; others do vary greatly. Occasionally, the ideas about marriage are not in step with the times or consistent with the circumstances. To evaluate your ideas about marriage, and the ideas other people have, we must look at marriage from the social scientist's point of view.

2

The Social Science View of Marriage

> The proper study of Mankind is Man.
> —ALEXANDER POPE

Social scientists also have ideas about marriage, just as you have, and their ideas come from careful study of human behavior in all times and places where human beings have lived together in large and small groups. For the social scientist, marriage is not so much something to be defined as something to be analyzed, in its many forms and variations. To arrive at an understanding of the universal characteristics of marriage, the social scientist goes back to the beginning of mankind as a species of animal different from all other species.

Human beings from the very beginning have paid a price for their unique ability to walk upright, on two legs instead of four. That price is the constriction of the female birth canal, which means human beings must be born before they achieve the level of maturity and self-reliance that most other animals reach before they are actually born. If they were as mature as most other animals at birth, they would be too large for the narrow human birth canal.

After birth children are absolutely dependent on adults for a long time. Usually, they don't walk until they are at least a year old. As a matter of fact, human babyhood is largely a being-carried period. Babies rather enjoy it and frequently voice their resentment over not being carried. It seems likely that prehistoric and modern babies are alike in this respect. It also seems likely that human mothers have always found baby-carrying something of a nuisance, and mothers of our very early ancestors found it to be a matter of life or death.

Mothers couldn't hunt for their own food very well while they toted an infant on their backs or in their arms. They couldn't defend themselves against wild animals and other enemies. They couldn't go long distances to gather firewood. In short, they needed a man around the house—or the cave. It seems reasonable that the man who assumed these duties should be the one who was responsible for the infant in the first place. But early man had his problems, too. If he went very far from home alone in his search for food or game, he left the woman and child defenseless and more or less helpless.

Another penalty that man pays for the ability to walk upright is his vulnerability. His vital organs are essentially exposed, even when he wears clothes. Furthermore, his strength is less than that of most of his prey. He compensates for this comparative weakness by his ability to reason out the relationship between cause and effect. That is why man is called *homo sapiens* ("thinking man"). Using his power of reason, early man developed the idea of co-operation with other men, all working together for mutual protection and for production (or collection) of the necessities of life.

Each person living in a group had his own specialty or occupation for which he was best fitted. This arrangement constituted a society. In addition to designating specific tasks to individuals, the society also made certain rules and established laws to preserve the integrity of the group. It was not enough that some men hunted while others carved or made tools. The small society which a man and woman established when they had a child, or children, had to be made firm and more or less permanent so that the woman could count on the return of the man from whatever wild-goose chase he made. This was necessary because of the helplessness of the babies, and also by the economic factor of property ownership, whether it involved only rudimentary utensils or parcels of land. So the social institution of marriage developed.

By law, custom, and accepted tradition marriage kept a man and a woman together at least long enough to make sure that their children could shift for themselves. Century after century all over the world, marriage has acquired clusters of values that surpass the utilitarian assurance that the man of the family would return home more or less on schedule. The values have not always been the same, and the marriage patterns differ with time and place. But some fundamentals have been universal.

First, although various societies have had differing views about permitting sexual gratification outside of marriage, most have recognized that sexual promiscuity is detrimental to the welfare of everyone in the society. The institution of marriage, regardless of its form, and regardless of customs permitting multiple wives or husbands, has always exercised control in one form or another over the sexual activity of both men and women.

Second, all societies link marriage with economics. The continuity of ownership of property or wealth is always linked with marriage, directly from husband to wife or vice versa, or through the children resulting from marriage. Societies see marriage as a way of ensuring the economic support of individuals. In general, husbands support wives (although today the arrangement is sometimes reversed), and wives, in turn, help husbands both by helping to make the support possible and by maintaining the home.

Third, marriage universally has been a means of satisfying some emotional needs of human beings. The fact that in individual instances it has sometimes failed in this respect does not alter the basic truth. Mankind has always thought of marriage as providing for both partners a feeling of security, companionship, identity, and affection or love.

At this point the phrase social institution should be explained. In living together people develop recognized and accepted ways of doing things, which we call social institutions. These involve expectations of certain kinds of behavior, which are expressed in the form of customs, traditions, and laws. For instance, our society expects a father to provide for his family, and there are laws expressing this expectation (concerning alimony, for example). As the need for certain types of behavior changes or disappears, social institutions may change or die out. Among those that have survived countless changes throughout the centuries are the family and marriage.

A possible formal definition of marriage as a social institution reads like this:

Marriage is a three-way agreement between society, a man, and a woman, providing that the man and woman may live together more or less permanently in order to satisfy their sexual, emotional, and material needs, and to provide for the welfare and development of their children.

The essence of this definition is its emphasis on society's part in the marriage contract. It must always be remembered that marriage is more than a private arrangement between a man and woman. Marriage under any circumstances, in whatever culture, must be sanctioned by society, and marriage can be dissolved only by permission of society. Societies may exercise further authority through laws, customs, or traditions, and these are enforced by a variety of attitudes.

Although all societies recognize marriage as a social institution, they do not all agree on its specifics or forms. This is particularly evident in regard to the number of spouses various societies permit. There are, basically, three different kinds of marriage relating to this factor: polygyny, polyandry, and monogamy.

Polygyny is a form of marriage that allows a man to have more than one wife—sometimes as many as he can afford to support. The opposite of polygyny is polyandry, which permits a woman to have more than one husband. The form we have in America is monogamy—one wife and one husband at a time. (Of course, reports of rapid changes of marriage partners in centers like Reno and Las

Vegas sometimes suggest a very fine line of distinction.) But monogamy is by no means the standard form of marriage throughout the world.

The ideas about marriage held by social scientists are based on concepts regarding what are called position, roles, status, and norms. This terminology makes it much easier to discuss the subject, if the terms are clearly understood.

The word "position" is used to indicate the place a man, woman, or child holds in a social structure. For instance, there is the basic position of being male or female. This position is entirely a matter of birth, or chance. At the same time, however, a man may also have the positions of husband, father, and storekeeper. A woman may also have the positions of wife, mother, and teacher. A child is either a son or a daughter, and may be a brother or a sister. Some positions may be determined by socio-economic class, race, or ethnic background, but although these positions are relatively stable, they can change with time, depending partly upon the individual himself and what he does in regard to the basic positions he holds in the social structure. The whole idea of position in the social structure is based on placing people in the social structure. This means that for every position there has to be a counter-position in the social structure. A husband has to have a wife, and vice versa. For another example: a father or mother must interact with a child in a way appropriate to the child's sex. There is the position of father of a daughter, or mother of a son, and there are also the counter-positions of being daughter or son to a father and a mother. You can make quite an interesting game by pairing positions and counter-positions for practically every basic social situation you can imagine.

What a person is expected to do and how he is expected to do it, in each of the social positions he occupies simultaneously and in succession during his lifetime, are called "roles." Each separate expectation of behavior is called a "norm." We differentiate between position and role because position is relatively stable and fixed, whereas roles associated with a given position fluctuate with time, place, and the general culture. The so-called "generation gap," widely discussed today, is an example. The positions of father and mother are the same as they always have been, but the roles and norms associated with these positions, both for the individual and society itself, are different from those of a generation or so ago.

"Status" is another concept necessary to understanding the social science idea of marriage. Status is a sort of composite indicating the position and the role along with the relative importance that society or the individual attaches to them. This idea is of paramount importance in marriage. The following incident illustrates the concepts of position, role, and status.

> A citizens' committee is meeting to discuss needs of the community and state. The chairman asks committee members to introduce and identify themselves. They go around the table in turn. One represents a labor union; another is a representative of the Council of Churches; there is a professor from the state university, and an officer of the local bar association. And so it goes until we come to Mrs. Jones. She is a rather self-effacing person, quite attractive, but a bit mousy. When her turn comes, she says, "My name is Martha Jones, and I am just a housewife."

This statement identifies one of the roles connected with Mrs. Jones's position of wife in the social structure. Since she is present at the meeting of the committee, she is not only a wife but also a community representative. She has at least two positions and two sets of roles to play, but the words she used in identifying her position convey the idea of the importance she expects other people to attach to it. When she says, "I am *just* a housewife," she is establishing not only her position, but also her status.

Her idea of the importance of her position may not be the same as the ideas of the other committee members. The chairman, whose role is complementary to that of committee members, may say, for instance, "Well, Mrs. Jones, we're glad to have you on the committee because we value very much the opinions of housewives." Secretly, Mrs. Jones may feel that her position is important and significant, even though she pretends to play it down. Status, then, is a term indicating implications of the importance of a position—as viewed by both other people and the person who occupies the position.

Social scientists find there are a number of roles associated with the basic positions of husband and wife. They have to do exclusively with the husband-wife relationship and interaction. The basic internal roles are:

1. Provider (supplier of food, shelter, clothing, etc. In some societies, this has also implied "protector.")

2. Helper (assistant to the other marriage partner)

3. Housekeeper or homemaker

4. Decision-maker

5. Companion

6. Lover

7. Sexual partner

Most husbands and wives eventually occupy the positions of father and mother (8). There are many roles accompanying the status of parent. The husband and the wife each occupy a variety of other positions, which have their own accompanying sets of roles and norms. These influence the relationship between themselves and others. For example:

9. Employee
10. Neighbor or friend
11. In-law
12. Married citizen

From the social scientist's point of view, the key to understanding how the parts and components of marriage work together is found in the way the basic positions and sets of roles are assigned to husband and wife, and how each plays the roles involved. Some of the roles are shared, as when both husband and wife are providers. And, of course, they both may be parents. One, however, is a father and the other is a mother, so parenthood is divided into two positions. The roles necessary to these positions may vary from one society to another and from one family to another, but a specific society, large or small is likely to have individual ideas about how the roles should be played. This leads back to the term *norm*. Again, the norm is what the majority of a social unit considers best or practices most commonly. All through the preceding list there are many interlocking positions and roles and norms. The interlocking patterns are influenced by such factors as

1. Race
2. Ethnic origin
3. Religion (sometimes)
4. Social class
5. Stage in the marriage cycle

The average American marriage lasts about forty years, unless it ends in divorce. Sociologists divide these forty years roughly into four periods, not equal in length, by any means. Each is very definitely separate, and different in the ways in which the positions and roles work together.

The first stage, called the "period of establishment," is the time between the wedding and the birth of the first child. This is the time when the husband and wife are learning how to fit together all the parts of marriage and how to assign and play the internal and external roles. For this reason, it is sometimes called the "period of adjustment." The emphasis is on the roles of lover, sexual partner, helper, and (probably) provider.

In the modern world, the period of adjustment may be complicated by the fact that it coincides with and overlaps the second stage of marriage—or, in all honesty, the classical basis for the second stage may actually precede the first.

The second stage of the marriage cycle, the "expanding-family period," begins with the birth of the first child, and lasts until the first child is grown up and goes off on his own. Here the emphasis is definitely on the roles of provider and parent. All the other roles are critical, though, because how these roles are performed tends to form habits that influence still later stages of the marriage. It is easy to slight these other roles in favor of those involved in being providers and parents, but actually they are important to the parent role, since children learn from their parents how to perform such roles as housekeeper or decision-maker.

When the oldest child leaves the parents' home, husband and wife begin the "period of the contracting family." The family gradually grows smaller and smaller until the youngest child leaves for his independent life. In this period, husband and wife may find themselves in the new positions of grandfather and grandmother, with new roles to play.

The last period of marriage is the time when the position of companion is specially important, and when the positions of grandfather and grandmother may be most engrossing. This means that the roles and norms concerned with the position of husband and wife, father and mother, are drastically changed. Also there is today more variation in the norms from one family to another and one society to another than has existed before. There are problems of economics, also. However, this stage of marriage is the one for which the preceding stages were designed. It is the combination of the whole saga of married life.

These concepts from social science will prove useful in the following detailed discussion of each of the ten areas of marriage.

3

Sex Roles

> So clinging vines, cling, make a man seem a tower,
> Be soft and be helpless, and frequently cower,
> Look up at him, even if two inches taller,
> And loosen his tie and unbutton his collar,
> Yet do all the cooking, the cleaning, the shopping,
> From sun up to sundown without ever stopping.
>
> In short, if you'd please Mr. Average Spouse,
> Be as strong as a moose and as meek as a mouse.
> —RICHARD ARMOUR: "Ideal Woman"

Underneath the surface of the simple definition of sex roles as the way people think, feel, and act as men or women, are some powerfully explosive implications. One is that the way people think, feel, and act as a result of being male or female may not be the way society expects them to. Another, and even more explosive, implication is that a value judgment may be called for. Are males superior to females, or the other way round? Still another implication is the question of whether sex roles are naturally determined by physical, emotional, and intellectual differences between males and females. These and other implications of this definition make sex role ideas probably more important in marriage than any other factor, because they are involved in every one of the other nine areas of marriage.

It is natural to think that the basis of sex roles is the physical difference between male and female. Of course, this is quite true when the roles involve sexual activity, reproduction, and some aspects of child-care. There are still other physical characteristics definitely associated with being male or female that influence sex roles.

On the average, males are taller, heavier, and more strongly muscled than females. On the other hand, the average woman has better control of the fine muscles to do work like sewing and sorting out small articles. Men are often physically more active, more inclined to games of all sorts, and more aggressive than women. Women are more likely to be patient with quiet sitting while they do routine work. In general, they are more interested in grooming than men. They are more affectionate. They tend to let men take leadership in most affairs. Many people believe these sex role characteristics are genetic and are shared by other animals, including man's closest relatives, the apes.

In the area of intelligence, which should play a part in determining some sex roles, the facts are not entirely clear. Each sex, on the average, is so much smarter than the other in some respects that no comparison is possible. For instance, the standard IQ tests indicate that girls are better than boys in the parts of the test that involve matching of colors and shapes, memorizing things, use of language, and anything reflecting a "social science." On the other hand, boys are better than girls at abstract reasoning, mathematics, and mechanical ability. When standardized tests were first being developed, questions and problems that resulted in very marked sex differences in the scores had to be eliminated from the tests in order to get results that would make the IQ's at all compatible. The result was tests that are deliberately stacked so that neither sex can have an advantage over the other. They prove nothing about the relative intelligence of males and females.

The relative intelligence and comparative "intelligences" of male and female lead to the very heart of how sex roles are determined. Using school grades as an indicator, statisticians have found that in the elementary grades girls tend to get better marks than boys.

When they reach high school, boys catch up and do better than girls, on the average. When they go to college, the boys have a clear lead over their female classmates. Yet there is no scientific proof that males become smarter as they grow older, or females less smart. What, then, causes the difference in scholastic performance? One possible answer illustrates how sex roles can be determined by society and culture, despite the natural differences between male and female.

A possible explanation of the progressive downward trend of school grades earned by girls may lie in a deep-seated cultural belief that men *should* be more intelligent than women, because traditionally husbands are providers and women are housekeepers. Perhaps people tend to think that providing requires more smart thinking than housekeeping. If this suggestion has validity, women may believe that men don't want to marry women who are more intelligent than they. It is at least possible that the downward trend of female grades may indicate an unconscious motivation for some females, in statistically significant numbers, to display less intelligence than they actually possess. This possible answer is suggested entirely for its illustrative value; it has no scientific basis.

The fact is that, despite genetic differences between the sexes, society does create and more or less enforce differentiated sex roles. The roles are usually geared to specific needs of the people who make up the societies and are enforced by status. An interesting example is found in Eskimo culture, where the men hunt seals in kayaks on the open sea. For protection against cold and wet, they wear leather clothes, which become stiff and dry. One sex role of wives is to chew the leather garments, in the evenings, to make them soft and pliable when the men don them for the next day's hunting. Older wives who have performed their roles well have worn their teeth down to stubs, thereby gaining status among the other wives as well as among the men.

Society determines the roles in accordance with its needs at a particular time and place. In general, many of these sex roles have, over the centuries, resulted in sex-associated attributes that sometimes seemed so fixed that people thought of them as inherent. The discovery that they are not has influenced marriage profoundly. An extract from Margaret Mead's book *Male and Female* tells about changes in some aspects of American marriage brought about by the needs of early American and frontier life.

> . . . The valuation placed on female qualities shifted. Meekness, home-abidingness, timorous clinging to the saddle of a husband as he rode away for a two-mile journey, were all very well in the Old World. But an American frontier woman might have to keep a lonely farm going all by herself for weeks, disciplining the half-grown children, succouring the passing stranger, even fending off the Indians. Strong women, women with character and determination, in fact women with guts, became more and more acceptable. . . . Along with this demand for women who have strength of character and the ability to manage money and affairs, there went no parallel premium on women's looking masculine. A woman was still expected to have womanly qualities, still to be attractive, in fact she was expected to be increasingly attractive, as she came to be chosen in marriage for her dowryless self alone. Marriages of choice, phrased as marriages of love, laid increasing demands on both men and women to please the opposite sex openly.
>
> In the hurly-burly of settling a new continent, many tasks were delegated to women in addition to running the farm and disciplining the children and keeping off the Indians while their husbands were away. As rough little frontier settlements assumed the appearance of a real village, the cleaning-up process, closing down the gambling-hall or the saloon, was thought of as coinciding with the arrival of one or more good women. The finer things of life—moral and aesthetic values—were delegated to women in a new and more active form; America was not Europe, where women had been expected to

SEX ROLES

> *do more praying than the men but not to take any responsibility outside the home* . . .[1]

This statement shows how new and changing roles for women also affected their status. The changing status of women, based on new roles, has been going on since the earliest days of American history, and has been copied in other societies throughout the world. Males in almost all cultures have had higher status than females, and most societies are loath to change the situation. The problem is to raise the status of women, along with changing roles, without lowering the status of men. The movement is toward a balance of sex-based status by adding more on the female side without taking anything away from the male side of the point of balance.

The status of women as wives has always been rather high. But, until comparatively recent years, this status was based first on the simple fact of marriage itself. Marriage has always conferred status, but the roles involved were chiefly those of wife and mother.

Gradually, in America first and then elsewhere, women have been allowed to play more and more of the roles connected with the twelve internal and external positions listed in the preceding chapter. The positions most involved are those of provider, decision-maker, and member of society at large. This has given new statuses to women that affect marriage. Remembering that the right of American women to vote was not achieved until 1920, you can get some idea of how this works from the following editorial—along with a sidelight on some of what we discussed in the preceding chapter.

SWAZI MATRIARCHY

> Self-government has its troubles in variety around the world. For example, consider the situation in Swaziland, tiny British protectorate in southeast Africa, which has just elected a government expected to lead it to independence by 1969.

---
[1] Sources are listed beginning page 169.

Swaziland has women's suffrage, and then some. In prior elections, one wife per family was permitted to vote. But that policy had caused such disruptions in Swazi's polygamous households that, for this month's election, the government ruled that all wives could vote. Many Swazis have six or seven wives. King Sobhuza, head of state, is reported to have fifty.

The wives thus have an assured majority in Swaziland, and the League of Swazi Women Voters probably has one issue high on its list for action: Polygamy [polygyny] *with the male the master cannot survive where women make the laws.*[2]

The Swaziland situation illustrates in some ways what happened in the United States with the adoption of women's suffrage half a century ago—without, of course, the involvement of polygyny. In the last fifty years, there have been other and more drastic changes in sex roles in America and elsewhere. Let's look at an essay that describes some of these and the problems in marriage they have created.

DILEMMAS OF A HOUSEHUSBAND

At table not long ago, one of our daughters announced she had solved a problem in school. The issue was a routine questionnaire which asked for "father's occupation." After considering the alternatives, she finally wrote into the appropriate space: Househusband.

The initial impact of her word-coinage brought general merriment to the three other females in our family—my wife and daughters. But this unexpected confrontation with our space-age dilemma caused me to lose some of the savor of my own home-cooking. . . .

I present this vignette:

A marries B. As college graduates, both are gainfully employed in their chosen fields. A earns almost twice as much as B. They produce three children, live in typical mortgaged sub-division two-car comfort. Then family responsibilities suggest that one person ought to be at home as a full-time parent and homemaker. So B leaves the work force to fulfill this need. . . .

Let me be more direct about this. I am B.

I am not in this predicament by accident. In an age of specialists, particular skills earn handsome rewards, while other talents may go begging. When I was a beginning teacher, my superior told me that with a doctorate beyond my master's degree I might aspire to a salary of over $9,000. At that time my wife was making nearly that much as a young electrical engineer. This was no surprise. When we married, with my college behind me and hers just about to start, we had selected a field which suited her talents and interests and the rewards of the economy. We did not plan our family, but we did plan to raise one. The prospect of two careers coupled with the responsibilities of parenthood did not dismay us then, nor does it now.

There have, however, been crises, most of them due to the conflicting demands of children and jobs. As our three girls grew, we tried all forms of caring for them. We took them to private sitters, to nursery school, had both young and mature women live in by the week, took them to neighbors by the day, and to grandmother when she lived near enough. There were assets and liabilities to each arrangement. It was often difficult for the girls to adjust. But there seemed to be little to be gained in their over-all welfare by cutting off two-thirds of family income just to have mother at home. (The good reasons why mother does not choose to be at home is another story.) . . .

The change in the cycle of family adjustment came about through an opportunity my wife was offered for a cross-country job transfer. The uncertainties of moving to a new environment, plus a lack of available market for my special skills, suggested to us an experiment in role-reversal. With very little financial adjustment it was possible to provide a full-time parent in the home. Children could have their friends in the house to play in the afternoons, a request that was not often granted before. Meals would be more leisurely and better planned. Sickness of a child would no longer trigger an emergency change of all plans. Mother's night classes or out-of-town trips would not interfere with the growing outside activities of the older girls. And for father there would be time for the sabbatical—unpaid of course—time to absorb the writings that are the raw materials upon which a teacher must feed.

Despite all the aforestated logic commending our arrangement, the experiment has not been successful. Mr. B still equivocates when friends ask, "And what are you doing now?" There is no inclination to say honestly, "I am a househusband." B discovers that in the tug of reason against emotion, reason is not always the victor. For example, reason persuades that:

> An apron is a device for protecting clothing. B prefers grease spots on his pants to being viewed by neighbors in even the most masculine of aprons.

> B should be pleased when door-to-door salesmen refuse to do business with any but "the lady of the house." Yet this somehow makes B feel inadequate.

> It makes no difference if financial obligations must be made in the wife's name, since the same bank account satisfies all. Yet when a credit reference is required B is awkward, almost apologetic in inescapable explanations.

There is no need to pile on additional examples as testimony to the cumulative negative effect that minor irritants have built up. . . .

The househusband *has yet to be defined in our culture. What is a* househusband*?*

Since there are as yet no dictionary definitions, let us create one by starting with the opposite number, the well-known "Housewife: n. a woman who runs a home and takes care of domestic affairs." (Webster's New World.) Merely removing the letters wo *will not suffice because we read into this definition far more than is stated. Are we willing to grant to the male the additional criteria which are implicit in the term "housewife?"*

First we ought to write able-bodied *into our definition. The community approves of the working young-married couple. If children arrive and the couple continues to follow their separate careers they are likely to encounter genuine admiration, often expressed in some such declaration as, "Honestly, we don't see how you two manage it all!" Let the couple decide that it is to the best interests of the family for one of them to concentrate on the home during the critical child-raising years, and friends and neighbors will not only understand but applaud the wisdom of the decision. However, if the able-bodied, employable male should elect to be the one to interrupt his career, the community reaction will be negative. Men do run households—but they run them out of necessity, not choice; usually because of some disability which removes them from the work force.*

The second qualifier we must add to our definition of househusband *is* choice. *The fellow who chooses to trade places with the traditional little woman must be either sick or, worse, lazy. "Man you really got it made!" Our service station operator tells me with just a hint of friendly disapproval. Neighbors accept the deviation, but it is just that. Everyone, B included, looks for justifications and explanations that are not required of the housewife. Any adult member of the "weaker sex" is free to make a choice which is, in practice, denied her mate.*

33

Who is brave enough to accuse her of either debility or sloth in her appointed rounds?

The idea of the man in the home should not be as startling as it is. In the depression Thirties many an unfortunate husband manned the broom and pot while his secretary-wife brought home the bread. And is it not the male who dominates the commercial pinnacles of such feminine arts as fashion design, hair styling, decorating, and cooking?

Our family experiment suggests that the home isn't the place it used to be. In each family there is just about the same work to be done. Clothes must be washed and ironed, dishes scrubbed, lawns mowed, automobiles maintained. Children must be fed, dressed, supervised, counseled, and consoled—as well as ferried about to library, chum, or store. And someone must bring in enough money to meet the first of the month with at least a faint smile. What we are concerned about is not what must *be done*, but *how the workload is divided*.

Have our standards kept up with our technology? Remember the wringer washer with its drainage tubs to empty. Remember even the scrub brush, corrugated tin board, and yellow soap. Washday once required both muscle and stamina (and men let the women do the job.) Today Mr. B puts the load in the machine and shuts the lid. His work, the vital function, is executive—he must decide the correct choice of water temperature in wash and rinse, the timing of the cycle, the amount of water, the proper combination of compatible items to be washed. . . .

In the home of 1965 there is not much that can be justified as the exclusive domain of either sex. The army taught me to sew and to make a bed that will bounce a quarter. Why not put these skills to civilian use? The answer is that based on common sense we divide the *household tasks according to preferences, not gender. What household does not have such an arrangement? It is only when the role-expectancy factor becomes involved that conflicts develop. When the woman decides to leave the home, or the man options to abandon the business world, the fabric of environment and preconditioning cries out against it.*

Under the existing mores it is as difficult for the husband to invade the wife's house as it is for her to retire from it. It is this realization, especially if she is concerned for the welfare of her children in the interweaving of two working worlds, that prompts the capable young woman to hesitate committing herself to the arduous training leading to the professions. Without the active support of family and husband, her choice may well be career or marriage. There is no fundamental reason why she cannot have both.[3]

In this essay, there is reference to the effect of mechanical housekeeping aids. Let's pursue this a little further, because it has a peculiarly interesting influence on sex roles in marriage.

Today women theoretically have time to occupy more of the basic positions in the society of marriage than they once had. Some they can share with their husbands; others they can take over more or less completely. True, there are times in the marriage cycle, particularly during the early parts of the period of the expanding family, when the demands of the mother roles will limit the time. Nevertheless, women can have careers, even though married, and thus develop new sex roles in marriage and provide for personal development as human beings as well as wives. This is one effect of gadgets on sex roles. But there is another and more immediate effect of household gadgets and machinery on sex roles. Along with changes in economic structure and conditions in modern society, they have created what amounts to a new role—"repairer."

Keeping house is no longer a matter of cooking, cleaning, and making beds. Modern housekeepers, male or female, have to be jacks-of-all-trades or millionaires just to maintain the house. The more gadgets and labor-saving devices we have, the greater the necessity for keeping them running, and it is either very expensive or virtually impossible to get outside help in doing this. Many wives have abandoned the traditional sex role of mechanically helpless female and taken over some aspects of what was formerly the exclusively masculine role of repairer.

There was a time when a wife might lose status in the eyes of her friends and neighbors if she did repair chores culturally reserved for her husband, and her husband would lose status by allowing her to do them. If it happened that some of the chores assigned to the husband were not actually done, he lost status and his wife gained sympathy. "Poor woman! Her husband's so shiftless."

Today, wives sometimes seem to gain status by doing some of the jobs once entirely reserved for husbands; and conversely, the husband does not appear to lose status by letting his wife take over some of his traditional chores. A college professor tells this anecdote, which illustrates the point:

"You know, a strange thing happened to me recently. I didn't have any classes that day and so I was at home pecking away at the typewriter, trying to produce an article. I looked out of the window and I saw the woman across the street examining the street light in front of her house. (The houses in this area don't have regular street lights on tall poles. Instead each house has its own short light post and a contraption that turns on the light when its dark enough and turns it off when it's light enough.)

"About a week before, my own light had gone on the blink and I had spent two hours getting it back in operation; so I was interested in what the neighbor woman did. Well, she went back into her house, came out with a screwdriver and a pair of pliers, and attacked the lamp like an old pro. She unhooked all the wires, took the entire business apart, and fiddled around with the insides; and then she put it all back together again. Within thirty minutes she had it working in great shape.

"After that she put her tools away; pulled out the power lawn mower, started it expertly, and cut the grass. As I thought about this, it occurred to me that it had never once crossed my mind to say to myself that her husband must be a queer sort of duck not to have taken care of these two jobs himself. I don't know him personally; but he is obviously not a traveling man; he is home every day and every evening as far as I can see; and, from other things that I have seen him do, I believe he is perfectly capable of repairing lamps and mowing lawns. But I suddenly realized that what I had seen didn't violate my idea of the normative role for a wife."

This story illustrates what we might call the "new housewife." She paints houses, washes cars, makes kitchen cupboards—in fact, she does almost everything that used to be thought of as man's work in our society. There are, of course, physical limitations where sheer muscular strength is involved, but not as many as traditional cultural norms have assigned. This role, of course, is well-known to farm wives, and was known in pioneer days, as Margaret Mead suggested.

It is also true that there are class differences, and racial differences, in the acceptable norms for wives' encroachment on their husbands' work. But research indicates rather definitely that these class differences are being blunted in our modern world.

Of course, labor-saving devices aren't the only reason for an increase in the number of working wives. Other reasons are economic necessity for many people, an increase in the available jobs that women can do, and changes in education that make it possible for more women to do jobs they weren't formerly prepared to do. In any event, the working wife represents a change in sex roles second to none in the last century. One writer says, ". . . the time is rapidly approaching when paid employment (for wives) will be a practically universal experience at one point or another in the family life cycle. The old taboo on work for married women has been thoroughly demolished. Even wives who don't work nowadays usually feel that they could if they wanted to." [4] It is very likely you will either be married to a working wife or be a working wife yourself. And you have probably heard so much about the "problem of the working wife" that you expect some difficulty.

Since women first began to work outside the home in really significant numbers, social scientists have frequently studied the subject of working wives. The results compiled by these researchers are so contradictory it is unsafe to draw any final conclusions from them.

Research emphasizes the importance of the wife's satisfaction with her outside job. If she dislikes it and does her work only because she feels she must, then we begin to encounter the traditional problems of husband-wife relationships and the effect on children. The cause, many researchers believe, is not the fact of the wife working, but rather her dislike for the kind of work she does.

Some wives apparently feel they have to make a choice between two evils. They dislike their jobs, but they dislike housework still more. Taking a job outside the home offers some escape, at least. Others may not dislike housework so much, but feel they don't really have enough of it to keep busy. If these women have no other interests, they take a job they dislike to escape boredom at home.

On the other hand, some wives like their outside work so much that the jobs become emotional necessities. A wife's dependence on her job is most likely to occur when she is qualified in a profession or in a highly skilled occupation. In this case, the wife is apt to make a career of her outside-the-home work. There are of course, exceptions to this situation. She may satisfy her need by part-time work in a field that otherwise would have been a career.

Sex roles also affect marriage by offering possibilities for what is called "role conflict." Role conflict, however, is possible in any area of marriage and in areas of living that affect marriage only indirectly. It may result from several different situations. The most basic is the one resulting from a person's occupying two positions simultaneously wherein the normative role of one calls for action or behavior contrary to the action or behavior called for in the other.

Suppose you were a traffic policeman. You chased a speeding car, stopped it, and found your wife was driving it. One of your roles as policeman calls for you to be very objective and stern and to write a traffic citation. But two of your roles as husband call for you to be gentle and protective, especially since you will have to pay the fine yourself if your wife is not working. Of course, ethically you know what you have to do, but it is difficult.

Another kind of role conflict may result from what might be called "role-reversal" so that societal norms are violated. The conflict here is between society and the individual. Suppose the househusband's wife had agreed with society and had wanted to play the housewife role as much as she wanted to play the role of career woman. Can you see the potential affects on the marriage?

Role conflict can result simply from the fact that either husband or wife basically dislikes some of the roles normally required in one or more of the central roles involved in the areas of marriage. For instance, there is role conflict for the wife who hates to keep house but has to perform the role of housekeeper.

Probably the most frequently encountered role conflict is seen where husband and wife have different basic ideas about marriage. The conflicts result not only from the perceived norms for his or her own roles, but also from the perceived norms for the other. An example already suggested might be a husband's disapproval of working wives on the basis of his idea that the normative role for wife is housekeeper, and that of husband is sole provider.

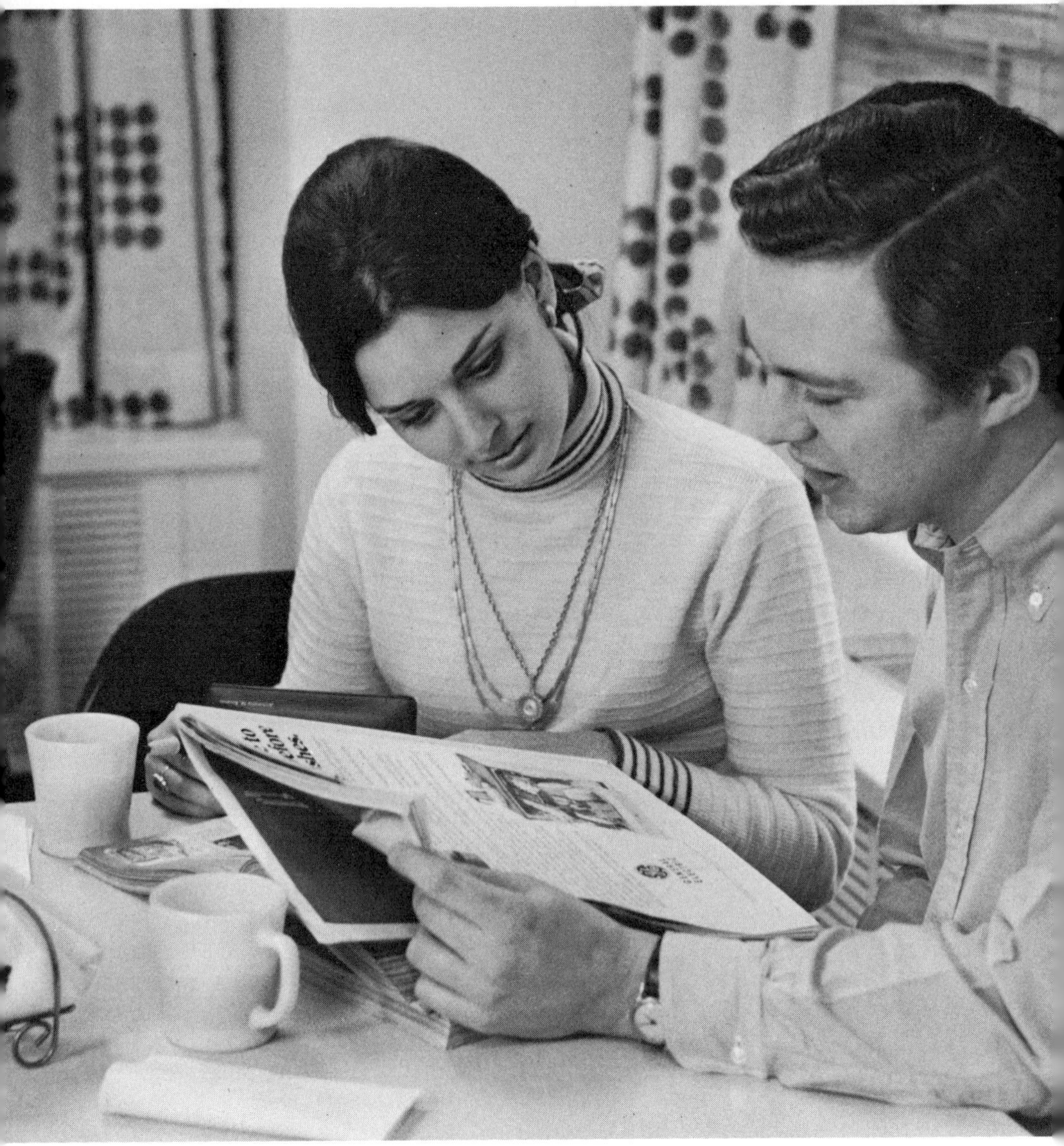

4

The Marriage Team

When the One Great Scorer comes to write against your name—
He marks—not that you won or lost—but how you played the game.
—GRANTLAND RICE: "Alumnus Football"

The area of marriage dealing with "authority," focuses on the external position of "decision-maker," which carries with it the power to make and to enforce decisions that affect the welfare of both husband and wife and their children. Societies have assigned this role to a variety of different persons and have designated a number of different norms associated with it. The American people represent cultures from all over the world, and consequently reflect probably more differing ideas about marriage than any other country. Despite this variety of ideas there is a more or less unified American way of handling the matter of authority in marriage.

The role of the decision-maker is not universally restricted to either husband or wife. In some of the older cultures in Europe and in China, for instance, the father of the husband carried out this role as long as he lived. In modern marriage in the United States and elsewhere, there is frequently no definite single authority in the hands of one decision-maker. Although this is not truly a universal cultural pattern, it is widespread and generally varies only with economic factors.

When sons are economically tied in one way or another to their fathers, the fathers may fill the role of decision-maker even though the sons are married. In older cultures, when sons were apprenticed to their fathers in a specific trade, the "father authority" pattern was common. Today the same circumstances can occur, and it is often true that the one who holds the purse strings makes the decisions. Generally, however, this situation is regarded as unhealthy.

Another pattern of decision-making vests virtually all authority in one or the other of the marriage partners. Culturally, when the father or mother of the married couple does not dominate, the decision-maker is usually the husband, in theory at least. However, the comic-paper cartoon of the henpecked husband is all too frequently accurate. That is, although the husband is officially the decision-maker, the wife subtly or by nagging actually makes the ultimate decisions.

A variation of this pattern provides that the decision-maker delegates to the other spouse responsiblity for making certain decisions in specific areas of their married life. This pattern has a number of drawbacks such as: role conflicts, dislike of role assignments, and inability in assigned roles. In addition, this pattern maintains the illusion of superiority of one spouse over the other. The final word rests with the chief decision-maker, who has the power of veto despite the theoretical division of responsibility according to areas of family living.

Because of this inequity, some marriage advisers have devised a pattern which is called "equalitarian marriage." This pattern theoretically gives husband and wife completely equal authority in making decisions affecting them both. In practice, this solution is more unsatisfactory than it is in theory. If husband and wife happen to agree completely, everything may appear to be rosy on the surface. But if they disagree, either there is a stalemate and no positive action is taken, or each of the marriage partners acts independently with potentially disastrous results for the marriage.

Despite all of these variations, however, there is an almost ideal arrangement, which has its roots in American history and has been

THE MARRIAGE TEAM

copied in many other parts of the world. This is the marriage team pattern.

The first permanent English settlement in our country was established in 1607 at Jamestown, Virginia. In the beginning all the settlers were men. They were not, however, confirmed bachelors. They wanted real homes, complete with good housekeepers and cooks. They wanted children to carry on the civilization they expected to build in the New World. In short, they wanted wives.

The only women in Virginia, however, were Indians. Despite the romantic story about Captain John Smith, a Jamestown man, and Pocahontas, who later married John Rolfe, most of the Indians were hostile and their women apparently had little to do with the Englishmen.

The Jamestown problem was solved in an ingenious way. The London Company, the group of Englishmen who had financed the colony, recruited unmarried women in England and sent them to Jamestown to become wives. Every effort was made to recruit only "decent" women, and women who were at least reasonably attractive. Probably few of these women had any romantic notions about what marriage offered them in the New World. The Jamestown excursion was, presumably, merely an escape from drab lives in England, where for one reason or another they had failed to get husbands.

Imagine their surprise, then, when they reached Virginia and found they could choose their own husbands. The choice was limited only by the supply of Jamestown men and the competition of other women in their group. In England their marriages would no doubt have been arranged by parents or some other third party, and they would normally have been expected to bring to marriage something in the way of a dowry, no matter how modest. None of these requirements existed in Jamestown.

Furthermore, since the supply of Jamestown men exceeded the supply of potential wives, the women found themselves in a very strong bargaining position. True, the men may possibly have rated the women on the basis of apparent ability to work hard, keep a neat and thrifty house and bear children and bring them up. But the women could demand something from their suitors that their English and European sisters weren't normally able to demand directly. They could use criteria of appearance, character, and behavior in selecting their husbands, just as modern American women do. Some elements of romantic marriage entered the picture.

This alone is enough to differentiate the first American marriages from most traditional Old World marriages, but there was something else, even more significant. It seems reasonable, in light of human nature, and because of her strong bargaining position, that a Jamestown wife could have demanded, and received, a voice in making decisions that affected both herself and her husband. There is no definite historical evidence about how standard this innovation was in Jamestown, but we know that it became more and more prevalent in other, slightly later colonies.

Elsewhere in early America, the marriage team concept was nurtured by other circumstances. All the first colonists, wherever they were, found themselves faced with the difficult task of managing to survive in a vast and hostile wilderness. They were thousands of miles and many weeks away from the source of supply for many of the things they needed to establish homes and lives comparable to, or better than, those they had left in the Old World. They had to become self-sufficient. It has been said that "the home was the factory during the first two centuries after our ancestors began to settle America." The home "factory" produced not only items to be sold but also items for daily use in the home and for clearing and cultivating the land for farming. Wives thus gained an economic importance regardless of whatever else they brought to marriage. They were valuable as workers in the home factory or farm. In a sense, husband and wife were frequently both marriage partners and business partners.

Another factor contributed to the development of the team concept in early America. In those days a young married couple could generally settle new land, move where opportunity seemed brightest, make their own decisions. If they wanted to be, they were "beholden to no one." There were always, in the beginning, new fields to conquer, and marriage became a symbol of independence. A Frenchman named Crèvecœur, who had lived in the middle colonies, had this to say about American marriage in 1775:

> *Every man takes a wife as soon as he chooses, and that is generally very early; no portion* [dowry or marriage price] *is required; none is expected; no marriage articles* [legal contracts] *are drawn up among us, by skillful lawyers, to puzzle and lead posterity to the bar, or to satisfy the pride of the parties. We give nothing with our daughters; their education, their health, and the customary out-set, are all that the fathers of numerous families can afford. As the wife's fortune consists principally in her future economy, modesty, and skillful management, so the husband's is founded on his abilities to labor, on his health, and the knowledge of some trade or business.*

Note what Crèvecœur lists as the bases for what was presumably regarded as "successful marriage": education, health, a few material goods, some idea of how to be economical, modesty on the wife's part, ability to labor, and the knowledge of some trade or business. With these combined resources, and free from the authority and dictates of elders, they made their own way as a marriage team. For these early American husbands and wives, marriage teamwork was largely a matter of laboring together to produce the necessities of life, although there certainly were emotional overtones. Benjamin Franklin, in his *Autobiography*, suggests the way things were in the eighteenth century. Concerning his wife he said, ". . . she proved a good and faithful helpmate, assisted me much by attending the shop. We strove together, and have ever mutually endeavored to make each other happy."

Independence of the married couple has become a sort of hallmark of American marriage. It has led to the development of what social scientists call "the isolated nuclear family." Although it has disadvantages as well as merits, it is certainly the basis for the development of the marriage team concept, which is concerned not merely with the way husband and wife work together to make their living, but chiefly with the way they make decisions.

Modern living is a great deal more complicated than living in Crèvecœur's or Benjamin Franklin's day. Modern marriage partners require a larger body of information and knowledge than they did two hundred years ago in order to plan ahead for themselves and their children.

Neither husband nor wife alone will be able to solve all the complicated problems they will meet. The modern marriage team is not a team for labor alone; it is a decision-making, policy-setting team, and a team to make the policies and decisions work the way they were planned to work. Decisions and policies are made and set in order to solve problems. The following example illustrates what this means in a practical way.

Jake Arnold is a salesman for a large paint company. His wife, Jane, does not work. They have two children—a boy ten years old and a girl six. They live in a rented apartment not far from Jane's parents, of whom she is very fond. Jake likes his parents-in-law.

One day the company offers Jake a new job as manager of one of their branch stores in a small town about three hundred miles away. The job would mean an increase in pay for Jake. The situation is a little unusual, however, because the company makes it very clear that Jake isn't being forced to accept the new job; and if he doesn't take it, he will still be in line for promotion and may even, eventually, become manager of the larger store where he works now.

There are many possibilities for action, depending on the ideas about marriage and the role norms of the Arnolds. One possibility is that Jake accepts the offer after thinking it over privately and without telling Jane about it until he has made up his mind. Another possibility is that he simply tells Jane about the offer and waits for her reaction. She may flatly say "no" because she wants to stay near her parents, or because she doesn't want to live in a small town. Still another possibility is that both Jake and Jane may simply accept the offer because, after all, it does mean more money.

If the team idea is in operation, however, the decision might be made along these lines:

Jake comes home and tells Jane about the offer. He says, "What do you think we ought to do, honey?" Jane says, "Well, we ought to think this through pretty carefully and get all the facts." "All right," says Jake. "You look into it. I haven't got the time."

Jane then calls the principal of the school the children attend and asks him about the schools in the town where the new job is located and what effect he thinks transferring the children would have on their education. She gets an estimate on the cost of moving and finds out about the housing costs and possibilities in the new town. She talks with her parents about how they would react to her moving away from them. She even reads some articles about the advantages and disadvantages of life in a small town.

Meanwhile, Jake inquires more closely about his future with the paint company. How much more would he make as manager of the store he is in now than he would make as manager of the small-town store? How long will it be before he can expect this promotion? What would be the future possibilities if he took the small-town job? Eventually, Jake and Jane sit down and discuss the whole matter, weighing all the factors carefully. What they decide represents the solution to a problem—whether or not to accept the offer. The decision also involves the establishment of a policy. Perhaps the policy is one of these:

1. The welfare of the children comes first.

2. "Opportunity only knocks once. Accept it when it knocks."

3. A leisurely life in a small town has more advantages than a busy competitive life in a city.

4. Close relationships with parents and parents-in-law are of the first consideration.

Of course, there are many other possibilities. The point is that the Arnolds do more than make a decision about accepting or rejecting the offer. They establish a guideline for making other decisions. If they say that the policy is to make the welfare of the children the first consideration, this will influence them when they make decisions about buying life insurance, moving to a new neighborhood, and countless other matters that might involve the children. The Arnold story makes it possible to apply role theory in seeing how the marriage team idea operates in the area of authority.

When the marriage team is actually in operation, and in the process of making decisions and setting policies, the husband and wife are involved in three complementary roles. One of these is that of *leader*.

The role of the leader is to begin a discussion by recognizing that a problem exists, and presenting the items that require decision or policy-setting. This was Jake's role in the illustration. Every team has a leader, whether he is designated or not. The leader is not the director; he is the one who brings out the best performance of the other team member. The leader may actually do most of the talking; but if so, it is to clarify the discussion by presenting the open alternatives and consequences.

It makes no difference, really, whether the husband or the wife takes the role of leader. In actual practice, the position is likely to be assumed by the team member who first perceives the necessity for a decision or for setting a policy. In the Arnold situation, it was Jake who got the offer of a new job, so he took the role of leader in the discussion. If Jane had seen that they had to decide about buying a new couch, for instance, she might have been the leader. But she might simply have stated the problem and let Jake take over as leader. In other words, the role of leader may alternate between husband and wife, depending upon the subject or topic involved, or by mutual tacit agreement of the team. It should be clearly understood that the function of the leader is not to make the decision, but to direct the discussion and make certain that it moves toward solution of the problem.

Another complementary role, which must be filled by both members of the marriage team, in turn, is that of *critic*. The role of critic is to challenge and evaluate the points made in the discussion, but not to render judgment about them. The critic is not a dissenter, not one who constantly objects, but one who looks for weak points in the discussion of both members of the marriage team, and perhaps suggests other ways of approaching the subject under discussion.

The third role is that of expert. It may be determined, in part, by traditional sex roles. Perhaps the expert on a decision involving the purchase of a new automobile, for instance, will be the husband, because, as a male, he may know more about mechanical factors than his wife. On the other hand, the expert in decisions regarding home decoration or furniture may more likely be the wife, unless there are special circumstances.

Sex doesn't really count in determining who will fill the position of expert as much as tradition would indicate. In the Arnold case, the position of expert included the role of gathering, digesting, and organizing the information on which the team decision is based. When Jane Arnold consulted the school principal, got estimates on moving costs, and read articles about the advantages and disadvantages of small-town living, she was enacting the role of expert on the decision-making marriage team. Jake could have done it just as well, but he didn't have the time.

The essence of the marriage team concept is mutual agreement between husband and wife about who plays what role on the team at any stage of the problem-solving operation. The role assignment is made on the basis of ability and knowledge, or the opportunity to acquire it, rather than on tradition-bound positions established by sex. You won't apply the principles of teamwork all at once, and, even if you tried, the person you marry may not even want to apply them. Knowing the goal, you will have to work toward it at your own speed.

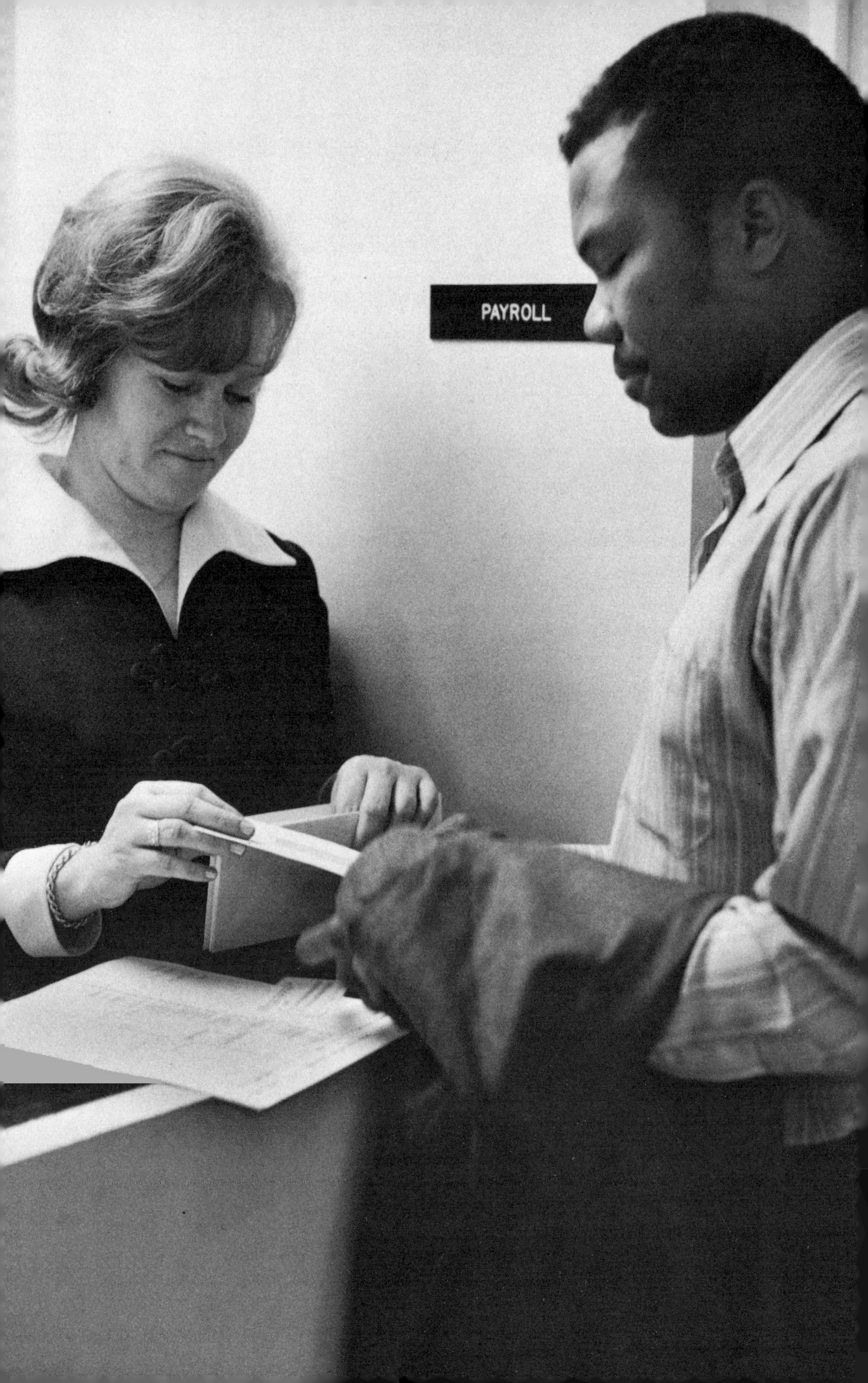
PAYROLL

5

Marriage Income

Getting and spending, we lay waste our powers . . .
—WILLIAM WORDSWORTH

A very high proportion of decision-making and authority problems in modern marriage involves the getting and using and saving of income. Most people automatically think of income in terms of dollars and cents from wages, salary, business, investments, or other sources. The key word is money, both getting it and spending it. But there is another way of thinking about income that applies to both the production of income and the use of it. In truth, this is the way economists think about income for a nation or city, and it is helpful in marriage, too. So forget about money itself for the time being and think of income as the total available and usable amount of goods, services, and satisfactions. Thinking about income in this way will help to explain why some people who have a great deal of money are not happy, and why some people who have very little money are happy.

Goods are the material items such as food, clothing, automobiles, television sets, washing machines, and hundreds of other tangible items that may or may not be as useful or necessary as these. But if the circumstances of life don't make these goods as important for some people as they do for others, the income is not actually reduced in this category.

Services are the jobs that have to be done by someone to keep life going on an even keel. The list is virtually unlimited. For illustration: cleaning house, washing dishes and clothes, repairing and maintaining certain goods, taking care of children or persons who are ill, haircutting and shampooing, mowing lawns, painting, etc. —it seems sometimes to go on forever. For some people, cash money is necessary for the production of this part of income; for others, money is not necessary in particular instances. But the services are still part of the total income.

Satisfactions are more difficult to describe in relation to the marriage team, because what may be a satisfaction for one may either not matter at all to the other or may actually be a source of dissatisfaction. But everyone needs the satisfaction of rest and relaxation, entertainment, and companionship. There are also satisfactions in dressing well, owning something unusual, carrying on a hobby.

We think of income as the total of all these three categories. One other factor that must be considered is time. The marriage team must think of income in terms of years rather than days. All decisions regarding income must take into account the future, the entire marriage and family cycle.

THE SOURCES OF INCOME. In the broad field of economics, natural resources like ore and forests are used to make goods such as steel and lumber, which in turn are made into houses, furniture, automobiles, and refrigerators. Water, another natural resource, is used to provide services like transportation and to make goods like electricity.

In much the same way, the marriage team has resources to provide the goods, services, and satisfactions that make up income. Like the natural resources of a nation, these must be recognized, used, and conserved.

Money itself is actually a means to an end rather than an end to be achieved. Nonetheless, we all tend to think of it as synonymous with income. For this reason economists, bowing to the popular conceptions, differentiate between "dollar income" and "nondollar income." For the marriage team, a balance of the two is essential in making economic decisions in terms of the three aspects of true income. It is regrettable that the word "income" is used in this dual way, but it is necessary in order to make the economics of marriage clear. This involves discovering, using, and conserving the team's economic resources in terms of both dollar and non-dollar income. These resources are greatly varied and they influence married life tremendously, especially in the area of satisfactions.

A resource is the reservoir, in terms of personal characteristics and money itself, from which the three parts of true income are drawn.

One resource, for instance, is the strength and energy of one or both of the marriage partners, and it varies from person to person and from one marriage team to another. Draining this resource can be economically dangerous. It has a number of other effects on the economic side of marriage. For instance if you are a woman, it may be a factor in deciding whether or not to be a working wife. Whether you are a man or a woman, it determines, in part at least, what occupation you enter to produce dollar income. It is also a factor in deciding how much non-dollar income you can earn. Strength and energy will eventually and inevitably be used up, so this resource is limited to the stages of life and marriage when it can be used.

What you know and what you know how to do are important dollar and non-dollar resources. The dollars you earn come from your ability to provide goods or services for which someone is willing to pay money. In general, the more you know the more dollars you make. This doesn't always seem to be true, perhaps, because sometimes one particular field of knowledge or know-how isn't as much in demand as another. For that reason, this resource is very important in making marriage team decisions that relate to economics. The team may have to decide whether one or the other should, for the sake of the future, use money and time to gain knowledge and know-how in a different field or to augment his ability in the present field.

Knowledge and know-how is also a vital resource for the production of non-dollar income. In fact, it is positively essential whenever there is a choice between dollar or non-dollar production of goods or services. Some satisfactions may not involve this resource so much, but knowing how to repair an automobile, paint a house, put up a shelf, fix a light fixture, plant a vegetable garden, and hundreds of other jobs around the house require that the marriage team decide whether or not to hire someone else to do them. The decision, of course, involves strength and energy as well as know-how. It also depends on available time, a third resource.

Of the twenty-four hours every day, some must be spent in sleep; some hours, or parts of hours, are used for eating, washing, brushing teeth, and attending to body functions. It's fair to say, however, that most people *can* use around fourteen hours a day to produce income. Time can be thought of as either a dollar or a non-dollar resource. Deciding which it shall be is one of the decisions the marriage team must make.

Money itself is an income resource. What is not used for goods, services, and satisfactions can be salted away and made to produce still more money for more income. It may be put into a savings account, where it earns interest, or it may be used to buy into a business directly or through stocks or bonds.

Even if you don't own stocks and bonds, other people's invested money can be an income resource for you through gifts or legacies from relatives. Moreover, it is from this kind of invested money that banks get the money they lend you. Loans and gifts may be considered as dollar income, but remember the time factor. Loans must be repaid, and gifts don't come forever on a regular schedule.

If you listen to the radio, watch television, or read newspapers and magazines, you know something about education as a resource for income. The trend is toward more and more formal schooling as a requirement for being hired to do almost anything. Education as an income resource, however, is not merely accumulation of information. The basic purpose of education is to develop the ability to see, understand, and think about the world in which we live. Education makes it possible for one individual, in the course of a lifetime, to profit by the experience and thinking of countless other individuals from the beginnings of time. Education cannot be brought up-to-date; it is a continuing process and is by no means confined to what one does in school or in college. Quite apart from the knowledge and know-how that education may provide, it also is a tremendous resource for non-dollar income in the form of satisfactions.

Community services such as police protection, the fire department and public health services can be considered income resources rather than merely conveniences or money-savers. Other community resources are public libraries, parks and playgrounds, state or local employment services and counseling agencies, and, of course, all of the agencies served by Community Chest or United Good Neighbor organizations. Although there is sometimes some expense involved, community concerts or theatrical productions, museums, and zoos are resources. The church, too, is a community resource which provides opportunities for a great deal of income in the form of satisfactions and services.

Where you live and the special features of your environment combine to make a resource for income. Mountains, lakes, forests, and the sea contribute to the environment and are resources. The kind of industry most common in the area where you live is part of your environment. Whether you live in a city or in the country determines another part of your environment, which includes your neighborhood and your family's home.

Perhaps the satisfactions of living on the seacoast, where you can watch storms, passing ships, and spouting whales, outweighs in non-dollar income the dollar rewards of living in the city. The environment of your place of work may produce satisfactions that affect your ability to work well and produce more, thereby influencing your dollar income production. That is why so many businesses and manufacturers are giving more and more attention to air conditioning, good lighting, and the beauty of offices and plants.

These are the principal income resources the marriage team must consider when making decisions in the area of economics. In practice the decisions are made by weighing dollar income against non-dollar income.

If your house needs painting, you have a choice between painting it yourself and hiring a housepainter to do it. If you need a new dress, you have a choice between buying one ready-made or making one yourself.

Both of these projects involve some expenditure of money. You will have to buy paint and brushes, and you will need a ladder and other equipment. You will probably ruin a couple of sets of workclothes, too, in the painting project. If you make the dress, you will have to buy material. You will need a sewing machine and other sewing tools. If the net cost of materials, equipment, and tools is less than the cost of buying a ready-made dress or hiring a housepainter, you can chalk up the difference as non-dollar income.

A power paint-spraying machine would help in the housepainting project. The power paint-sprayer just might be justified for one house-painting job, if its cost was less than the cost of hiring a professional painter. It would also have the advantage of saving time for some other dollar or non-dollar producing activity, as well as being a resource for future painting projects. Many other labor- and time-saving devices can be resources for non-dollar income, if they really produce greater efficiency and if the time they save is used for something that contributes to production of other income or resources.

So far we have thought of non-dollar income as an almost immediate substitute for dollars. That is, the activity can be given a dollar value in budgeting from day to day, month to month, or year to year. But you can think of non-dollar income in another way and see how the resource of time can be used to good advantage. Time used in building up the resource of knowledge and know-how can be considered as time spent in the production of non-dollar income, although the translation into dollar equivalent is deferred, perhaps, until a later time. You might use the community resource of public schools, which frequently offer courses in such subjects as upholstering or woodworking. Even if you don't have anything to upholster or any need for another table or chair right now, learning how to do these things through instruction and practice could be non-dollar income, since it would make it possible to save money or contribute to the household sometime in the future.

Non-dollar income, especially in its guise as do-it-yourself activity, which is very fashionable these days, has some pitfalls that may turn what looks like income into outgo. Take, for example, the attractive notion of the home vegetable garden.

There is usually no question about the difference in quality of vegetables raised at home and vegetables purchased from the produce department of a supermarket. Although there are many good reasons for having a vegetable garden, only rarely does it produce adequate non-dollar income. If you take into account the cost of seed or plants, fertilizers, insecticides, water, and all the tools and special devices so easily sold to the unwary by garden centers, you may find the cost of homegrown vegetables considerably greater than the cost of vegetables purchased from the market. In addition, one has to balance the value of the time spent in gardening against the question of whether or not this time might be more profitably used in some other kind of income production. This line of thought leads directly into the territory that concerns almost all young marriage teams—the production of extra dollar income.

Practically every young married couple either feels pains in the pocketbook almost all the time, or on occasion needs extra dollars for some special purpose. The constant pain may be caused by one of two things. It may result from improper management of dollar income, or from the fact that the couple's dollar income is not high enough to live on comfortably.

Sometimes the demands on dollar income are not merely those involved in buying goods and services. They may be part of the job itself—such as the necessity for a fairly high standard of dress, high transportation costs, lunch costs, or the need to take special courses or training. These things may result in increased dollar income in the future. Of course, the pains might be lessened by changing jobs; but perhaps the present job offers a bright future or is something the jobholder actually prefers doing, despite the disadvantages.

The occasional need for extra income might result from having to buy a new refrigerator, pay an unexpected automobile repair bill, or from any of a thousand and one other emergencies all too familiar to every married couple.

One way of meeting this need is to use the resource of gifts and loans. For the very young couple, especially if one or both are in school or college, there is sometimes the possibility of a kind of subsidy or occasional financial help from the parents of either or both members of the team. The wisdom or folly of asking for money from parents depends entirely on what kind of people both the parents and the young marriage team are. Of course, it also depends on the ability of the parents to furnish the gifts or subsidy. Assuming they are able to do so, will the young couple feel that in accepting help from parents they lose pride and self-esteem? On the other hand, will the parents feel that in giving this kind of help they are also acquiring the right to dominate and control the activities and plans of the couple?

Sensitive pride on the part of the marriage team may actually hurt the parents who would like to help, and consequently damage the family relationships. The married couple should realize, too, that under no circumstances is it likely that the gifts and subsidies can go on forever. In other words, they should guard against habitual reliance upon parents. However, the pattern of parental help for young married couples, especially today when people are getting married at an earlier age, is more and more common and has worked out entirely satisfactorily in countless marriages.

Loans make up another source of dollar income under special circumstances. Loans are a legitimate source of income for emergencies or for long-range needs such as education or investment in equipment or property which will eventually pay in additional dollar income. But loans in any considerable amount from parents are likely to have serious results, because the tendency is to put off repayment. To the borrower the word loan may smell just a little sweeter than the word *gift*; but to the lender it may have an unfortunate odor. He would probably rather call it *gift* in the first place and get a certain amount of satisfaction from having made it.

Probably, most marriage teams are chiefly concerned with making decisions about two other ways of producing extra dollar income: double-jobbing, and the wife's working outside the home.

Chronic pocketbook pain for young marrieds in these days of high living costs has resulted in a new kind of financial aspirin which can have some painful side-effects, although it works well for some people. It is often called "moonlighting," based on the idea that a person tries to handle one job during the daytime and another at night. The nocturnal aspect is not always involved, however, so the practice is more properly called double-jobbing. The double-jobber is usually the husband.

There are obvious objections to this practice. One is that the double strain of two jobs at once may jeopardize health, and another is that efficiency in one or both jobs may be seriously reduced. If this happens, the jobholder may very well lose one job or the other and be no better off, even worse off, than if he had not attempted double-jobbing at all. A further objection is that double-jobbing cuts down the time husband and wife can be together and interferes with the operation of the marriage team. All of these dangers are based on the assumption that the second job is a fairly regular one that takes the husband away from home and requires approximately the same number of hours as the full-time job, so that sixteen instead of eight hours of the day are used in the production of dollar income.

If it is possible to change circumstances so that these assumptions don't apply, some of the dangers of double-jobbing may be reduced. In fact, it is possible to see how a kind of virtue might be made of the necessity for it. There might be fringe benefits in satisfactions. If the regular job is confining and sedentary, double-jobbing might produce extra income in exercise and relaxation as well as in cash. A young schoolteacher who was a drum-major in his high-school and college days now gives baton-twirling instruction to children in his neighborhood in return for a modest but helpful dollar income. At the same time, he gets the satisfaction of keeping up his earlier interest, being in the fresh air, and getting some needed physical exercise.

Another man is a triple-jobber because of his extra knowledge and know-how. He is a barber by trade, but he is also an expert tile-setter and earns money on the side tiling bathrooms and kitchen counters. On top of that, he sells insurance both in his barbershop and at home. Still another man is both a master carpenter and a

SOME THINGS THE LADIES TOLD US [5]

AMONG WORKING WIVES GROUPED BY . . .		THIS MANY ARE WORKING FULL TIME	THIS MANY HIRE DOMESTIC HELP
AGE	% OF TOTAL		
18 to 24	9%	80%	2%
25 to 34	20	66	11
35 to 44	29	69	26
45 to 54	25	73	18
55 to 64	12	76	30
Over 65	2	62	35
CHILDREN			
None	20	83	14
Preschool	16	56	12
Elementary	29	63	23
Jr. High	19	63	26
Sr. High	23	72	21
College	20	77	22
FAMILY INCOME			
Under $5,000	9	69	13
$5,000 to $8,000	27	68	8
$8,000 to $10,000	23	69	15
$10,000 to $15,000	22	78	33
Over $15,000	10	78	43

MARRIAGE INCOME

AND THIS MANY GIVE AS THEIR MAIN REASON FOR WORKING:				
PAY OFF DEBT	BETTER LIVING	SAVING FOR HOME	CHILDREN'S EDUCATION	ESCAPE BOREDOM
24%	34%	28%	6%	8%
35	30	15	10	8
18	28	11	26	18
17	40	7	31	10
7	35	11	20	14
14	32	5	19	11
14	40	20	0	14
40	30	17	15	12
33	33	10	25	12
23	29	8	37	12
18	36	7	38	12
15	29	6	47	13
24	42	13	13	4
35	31	14	21	6
14	38	11	20	13
15	29	9	30	18
7	21	9	17	28

journeyman cement-finisher. This gives him a special advantage for double-jobbing, because builders like to have cement work done on weekends, when it doesn't interfere so much with other parts of the construction process.

One unusual illustration of a kind of double-jobbing, though it may not be widely applicable, is nonetheless provocative and may suggest infinite possibilities. A man and his wife who had taken a night class in ceramics—making things out of clay, and baking them in a kiln—eventually managed to buy their own equipment and continue the hobby at home, in the basement.

One Christmas they decorated their greeting cards with small ceramic seals. Everyone praised the idea so much they decided to make similar seals and sell them. The project is tremendously successful. The whole family participates almost all year round. There are six children in the family and each has a job on the "production line"—from the three-year-old to the eldest. They are making a good extra dollar income, which they divide this way: eight per cent goes to the children for spending or putting in their piggy-banks; twelve per cent goes to the father and mother; and the rest goes into a joint fund for the college education of all the children.

Double-jobbing for wives is more difficult than for husbands unless you think of it as something to do when not on the job as a housewife. A woman might get extra dollar income as a dressmaker, or by using some special knowledge and know-how in baking or pickle-making. Then, of course, there is the well-known home occupation of making telephone solicitations for business firms. For the most part, however, double-jobbing for wives means simply becoming a working wife—full or part-time.

THE ECONOMICS OF WORKING WIVES. Whether a wife works part-time or full-time outside the home, the economic truth is that the total net dollar income of the marriage team will not always be increased by the amount of her take-home pay. The reason is that working wives are apt to have more expenses related to their jobs than husbands, and this is especially true if they are mothers.

For instance, a working wife usually has more clothing expenses than her husband. Men can wear the same suit or set of work clothes day after day with alternations for cleaning. The working wife needs more variety of wardrobe. At least, custom and tradition dictate that the variety is essential. The working wife is apt to wear out more pairs of hose than the non-working wife and certainly more than the socks her husband wears out. She probably has more hairdresser expense than her husband has barber expense. If she is a mother, there are nursemaid or babysitting expenses. Also, she is apt to have less time for production of non-dollar income at home, so the dollar expense of living for the team is increased.

This is not an argument against wives working. It is simply a warning that, economically speaking, the total contribution she makes to the marriage team is not likely to be as great as she and her husband may think in the beginning.

In 1965 the magazine *Changing Times* made an informal survey of working wives. The precise figures have certainly changed and will continue to change, but the picture remains essentially the same in basic significance. Some of the facts are shown on pages 60–61.

Like her pioneer forebears, today's wife and mother is seeking the best the world has to offer for her family and herself. To get it, she may have to go outside the home, both for the money it will take to supply material needs and for the mental stimulus that will supply her own needs. In the *Changing Times* article, one mother summed it up this way:

"It may not be the easiest or most ideal way to live, but it has distinct advantages. Not the least of them is learning how to enjoy the time we do have together (wife and husband) and using it well. We try as a family to accept the difficulties we necessarily share and still find time for creative thinking and activity as the distinct individuals we are."

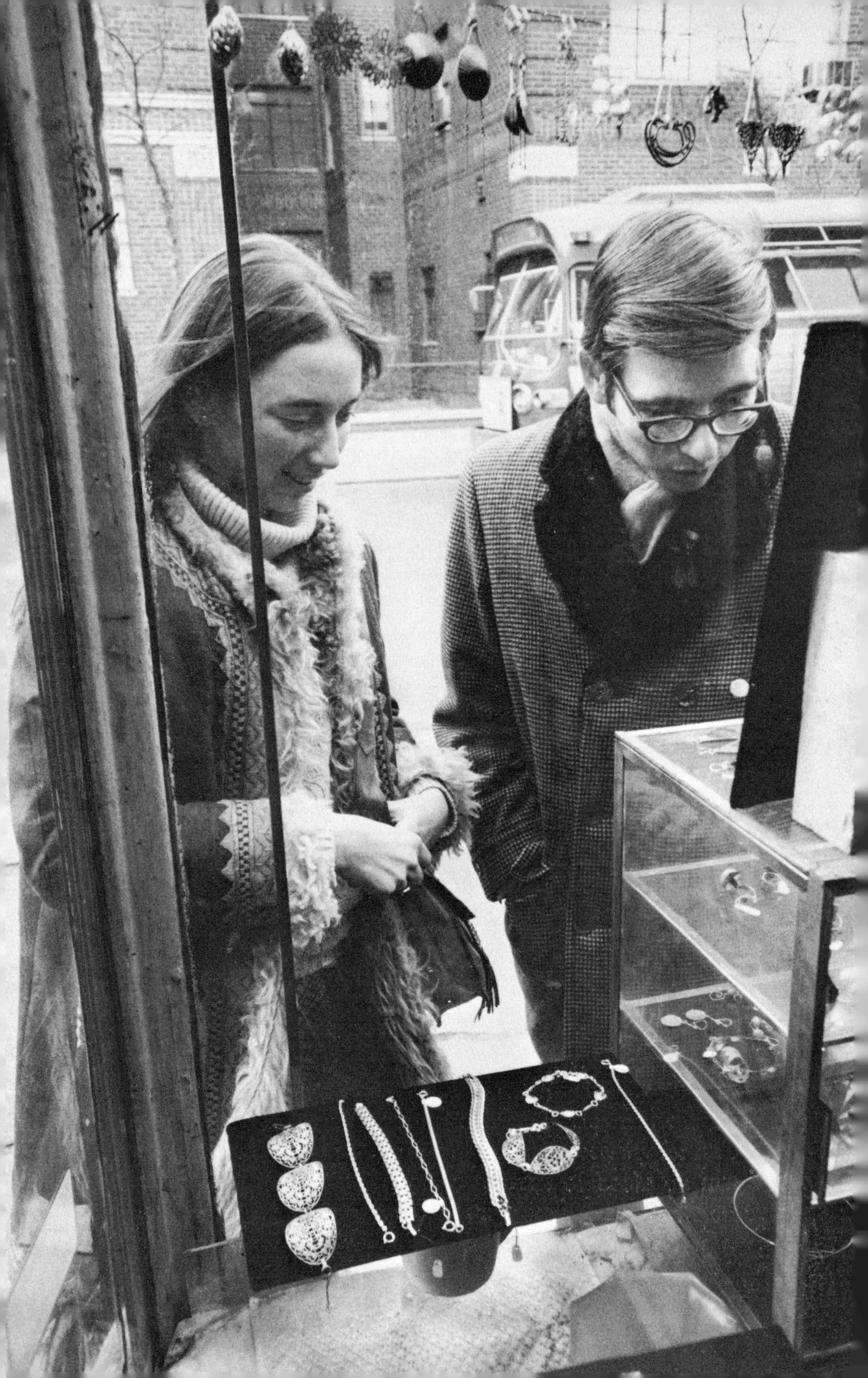

6

Money

> My wife insists that she and I
>   Keep separate accounts
> Of what we spend and what put by
>   Both large and small amounts.
>
> At keeping track of tricky sums
>   She's devilishly smart,
> And sees that, whatsoever comes,
>   Our cash is kept apart.
>
> Each month (there's nothing she prefers)
>   The checks and stubs she scours,
> To make quite sure that hers is hers
>   And what is mine is ours.
>   —RICHARD ARMOUR: "Method in Her Madness"

Even though money itself is not true income, it is extremely important in terms of the marriage team decisions. Getting and spending the dollar income is often a source of dissatisfaction and discord. Many studies of marital problems find money to be the basis of discord more frequently than any other single factor. The most frequent money-induced marital problem arises in answering this question: "Whose money is it? Is it yours, mine, or ours?"

The money we shall talk about is all the money both members of the team have, earn, inherit, or get from investments. It also includes property, such as real estate, that is a potential source of money. Husband and wife may have different ideas about how this money and property should be allocated, and each can probably find a historical justification for his views.

In the eighteenth century, Sir William Blackstone wrote his monumental *Commentaries on the Law of England*. This book became a basis of legal opinion and interpretation not only in England, but also in the United States, because our legal system is largely modeled on the English. In his book Blackstone wrote:

> *By marriage the husband and the wife are one person in the law; that is, the very being or legal existence of the woman is suspended during the marriage, or at least is incorporated and consolidated into that of her husband . . . Upon this principle of a union of person in husband and wife depend almost all the legal rights, duties and disabilities that either of them acquire by the marriage . . . For this reason a man cannot grant anything to his wife, or enter into a covenant with her; for the grant would be to suppose her separate existence, and therefore it is also generally true that all compacts made between husband and wife when single are voided by the inter-marriage.*

The law did allow a wife to keep whatever property she had owned before her marriage; but if this property included real estate, the husband was given complete control of the dollar income it produced as long as his wife lived. Dollar income then was the husband's—with no ifs, ands, or buts.

Of course, in Blackstone's day married women almost never worked outside the home for money. In general, women, whether married or single, had less education than men, especially in areas related to business. Moreover, property as a source of income was probably more important than it generally is today.

Farms produced almost everything farm families needed—food, wool for clothing, fuel, and most of the other basic necessities. When these were not all derived from the farm itself, there was always the opportunity to live off the land by hunting and fishing.

In the cities, equipment for carrying on a trade or business was the equivalent of land in the rural setting. Money, of course, did play an important part in the total scheme, but it was not as fundamental as it is today. Most services were supplied by the family itself and the satisfactions were implicit in the feeling of confidence in using the land and the equipment. Of course, money played a part in the total picture, but property was the real key, and the satisfactions were more simple than they are today. Sex roles were more definite, and the way they were played contributed to the satisfactions. Property was really the ultimate criteria.

There have been many changes since Blackstone's day. In the first place, wives are now definitely part of the dollar-income-producing team and decisions have to be made on this basis. Many states have community property laws that give the wife an equal share of all the property the couple gets after marriage, no matter who acquires it. She has the full right to make contracts, and is usually required to sign with her husband for legal arrangements, like mortgages, that affect the dollar income of the couple. This implicitly suggests that wives not only have the right but also the responsibility to participate in the management of dollar income as well as non-dollar income.

Another change is the fact that dollar income has largely replaced non-dollar income in marriage economy. Practically all the necessary goods and services *can* be purchased, and many of them *must* be purchased. Whereas non-dollar income was once paramount, dollar income is now the most important. As a result, more wives than ever before have become dollar income producers. This opens up a new way of looking at dollar income in marriage. Even if a wife doesn't work for pay outside the home, so many other woman do that dollar income management is seen in a different perspective from that of earlier times.

Many people, however, cherish remnants of the eighteenth-century ideas about money and marriage, whereas others have magnified the changes since then out of all proportion. The clash of the two extremes causes a great deal of difficulty in marriage that can be avoided if the marriage team concept is applied.

The marriage team concept rules out Blackstone and all his followers. It also rules out the most extreme ideas of those who dissent radically from Blackstone. The team answer to the initial question is: The income is ours—not because we are married, but because we are a team. We are individuals, and we shall work together in deciding how all the dollar income produced by each is used and conserved. We may end up keeping our incomes separate, or we may devise any number of other schemes for managing our income; but together we shall make the decisions and work out the schemes.

THE MARRIAGE TEAM METHOD. Approaches to the marriage team method are suggested in the following article by a well-known financial expert.

> If 1.8 million couples get married this year, there'll probably be only 1.7 million squabbles about money. Everybody doesn't argue over a dollar. But those who do won't get as much fun out of it as other generations did. There just isn't as much to quarrel about after taxes. There's more sport nowadays in joining forces, to peel every shred of profit off the take-home payroll.
>
> Statistics show that the number of marriages is rising, so maybe last year's 1.8 million will be topped . . .
>
> Certainly more of the young will have absorbed a better concept of money management, through various high school and college courses being taught these days. But even if the textbooks are forgotten, a couple of early decisions can help them off to a start in handling their incomes:
>
> The first is: What do you want your money to buy over a long haul? And secondly: How will you divide the responsibility for handling it—whether it's two paychecks or one?
>
> Agreement on these two points right at the beginning will serve to keep the temperature down when the bills go up.
>
> More and more young people are asking for suggested

MONEY

budgets to guide them in working out their own. All to the good. But remember that a budget with specific allowances for this and that will prove workable only if both husband and wife see eye to eye—not only on the figures but on the reasons why they're arrived at. So discuss, and delegate, these responsibilities:

Which salary, if there are two, will carry the weight of the savings program? If there's only one income, which marriage partner takes on the job of depositing the money and takes charge of the passbook? How will the checking account be set up?

It usually works out better if each partner has a separate checking account, even though in the early years of marriage a joint savings account is more practical.

Who will handle charge accounts at the stores? If she buys and he pays, a hassle can get going over a month's bills. Usually, the most harmonious method is to put one partner in charge, with authority to shop and the money in his or her checking account to pay.[6]

The positions and roles of the team have to be decided by discussion and negotiation. The central roles are as follows:

1. Cashier—handles the actual paying out of money and keeps records of what is paid.

2. Budget-planner—estimates future income and expenses and sets limits to expenditures in various categories.

3. Expert—knows as much as possible about the relative merits of goods and services that may be purchased, and keeps his information up-to-date.

4. Purchasing agent—does the shopping and the buying.

The team can work out any combination agreeable to both for playing the roles involved in these positions. It is possible that one or the other might occupy all four of them if both agree to the arrangement. It is also possible that some roles alternate between husband and wife or vary according to what the dollar income is used for. The essential point is that the positions and roles assigned by the team should match the abilities, interests, available time, and personalities of the role players. In the world of today, these are not necessarily determined by the accident of having been born male or female.

The team approach prevents the situation suggested in the following case (a wife is speaking):

> *"I was more of an executive type than Jim, so it was just natural for me to take the lead in making our decisions. I must have been too obvious about it, because the fellows in our group of married couples began to make jokes about his being 'henpecked' and about my 'wearing the pants.' Jim's reaction was terrific. He insisted on doing all the deciding. He took to ordering me about in the group. The worst thing about it was that his judgment was not as good as mine. Our family finances have suffered as a consequence. Worst of all, our happy relationship has become unhappy."* [7]

This case presents some interesting questions. What did the young wife mean when she said she was "the executive type"? If the couple had used the team approach instead of the individual approach, what would have been the basis of their team decisions? The answers to both questions are essentially the same.

The "executive type" carefully weighs present action against future consequences, and this is the primary basis for team decisions about the use of money. The advantages of the team method over the individual "executive type" method are that two heads are better than one, and the interrelationship of husband and wife is not damaged by apparent superiority of one or the other. In the case quoted above, there is an implication that if the wife had been in charge, everything would have been satisfactory, financially. Actually, the interrelationship would probably have been damaged as much as it was, but in reverse, since the husband would have been relegated to the inferior position.

Suppose, however, the money decisions are made by two heads instead of one regardless of whether one or the other or both are "the executive type." On what basis do they weigh the present against the future? This leads back to the stages of the marriage cycle outlined earlier.

In the period of establishment, the couple is "just getting started," and this age-old phrase means a great deal more than that they are just beginning to earn money. This is the stage when ingrown ideas about role assignments are most likely to operate. It is also the stage when money habits that will influence the succeeding stages are acquired. It is the stage for experimenting with some money-management procedures in order to find the best for the particular team.

Typically, the young couple is well aware that its dollar income is limited. The husband hasn't reached his maximum earning capacity; he has a lot to learn before he does reach it—either by more schooling or by experience. He may have to serve in the armed forces before he actually starts his learning. The wife probably works and contributes to the dollar income—indeed, she may provide all of it.

Some couples may expect to start living at least as well as their parents, forgetting that it may have taken their parents a quarter of a century to obtain the income, goods, and services that their children now take for granted. For most couples, however, the living requirements at the beginning are rather modest. Nobody expects them to live in a large or pretentious apartment or house, and in this period they don't need much room. They may eat canned spaghetti and beans rather than steaks and roasts, not only because it is cheaper, but also because it is simpler to prepare.

In the typical period of establishment, despite inevitable financial difficulties, there is apt to be an apparent, or real, margin between total dollar income and total dollar expenditures, regardless of how much or how little either is. This is where the executive decisions of the marriage team come into the picture in this first stage of the marriage cycle. There are no hard and fast rules governing these decisions. The only thing that can be said for certain is that, since these decisions are "executive" they must be made with an eye on the remaining stages of marriage.

The expanding-family or child-bearing period is relatively short, but the child-rearing period is a long one. It is divided into stages on the basis of the children's ages: pre-school stage; elementary-school period; high-school period; and possibly college period. Each of these stages has an individual pattern of expense. In the child-bearing and pre-school stage the medical expenses are apt to be quite high. In the elementary stage there may be expenses for fairly costly equipment such as bicycles and special clothing. High school usually introduces extra expense for food, transportation, and especially for girls, clothing.

Although money decisions throughout this period must be made with an eye to the future, they are usually based on what decisions in the first stage provided for living in this one. The husband's earning power is usually higher than it was, but the wife may be producing little or no dollar income. She is generally confined to producing non-dollar income. So the decisions center on ways of making sure that non-dollar income is adequate.

Depending on the decisions made in the period of establishment, decisions in the expanding-family period are likely to involve purchase of additional household equipment, continued savings, children's education, and daily living expenses. This is, without doubt, the most difficult marriage stage from the economic point of view. Even though dollar income may be higher, dollar outgo is also very much higher.

In the period of the contracting family, the expenses of child-rearing gradually diminish as each child leaves the home base. Food expenditures grow smaller (unless the general cost of living continues to increase), and, in time, cost of shelter may be reduced. But this period, like the preceding one, is also divided into stages.

The first of these may involve continued or increasing expense. Although this is supposed to be the launching period, when children become more and more self-sustaining, it is remarkable how costly the process can be. For many people the launching period actually involves a continuing education program in college, university, or vocational school, and the costs of education are growing by leaps and bounds. Also, the growing fashion of combining post-high-school education with marriage may increase the cost to the parents at a time that traditionally involved a slowly decreasing cost. Weddings are very expensive for the groom's parents as well as the bride's and usually under modern circumstances, whether or not the children continue schooling, there is the necessity of helping the young people get started in married life. And if, as so frequently happens today, the launching period also involves becoming grandfather and grandmother to the children of students still in school, the lauching period is really not a time to heave a sigh of relief. However, it usually is cause for hope that expenses will decrease in the next stage.

This is sometimes called the "period of financial recovery." This is the time when at least one of the parents is still employed and has probably reached maximum earning power. The length of this recovery stage is, of course, determined by the age of the parents when their children were born and the age at which they leave home.

The retirement or aging period puts all the income use-habits and all the income decisions, policies, and practices to the final test. Husband and wife must live on whatever retirement provisions they have made in the preceding stages of their marriage, in terms of all three kinds of income. The crux of the period is in that word *habit*. It applies to all periods of marriage, but it comes into focus most forcefully in the last period.

Early formed habits concerning the spending of dollar income may have to be broken. Habits of use of leisure time and other aspects of the earlier stages may, if they were well established, continue and be more important than they were originally. Since the habit-forming aspects of married life are important to all stages, as well as to the retirement period, it is possible to take an overview of the whole subject.

For instance, if the marriage team becomes accustomed to entertaining and being entertained a great deal, it will be difficult to break the habit even if it can no longer be maintained comfortably and easily. Eating out frequently is another habit that will probably have to be broken with the advent of the first child. You may have to spend some of your income on diapers and doctors instead of indulging the habit of buying a new dress every time you find a bargain.

However, denial of some of the satisfactions of life on grounds that they will be enjoyed later is not always the best policy. A great many marriages have failed because present satisfactions were forgone, theoretically to insure having them "in the future." But somehow "the future" never comes. The principle is the old one formulated by Aristotle centuries ago: "Of nothing too much!"—not too much denial of satisfactions, and not too much indulgence in them. Preparing for the future can be, in itself, a satisfaction. When it is not—when it involves miserable self-denial—it is a liability, not an asset. At this point interrelationships become especially important, and the idea of the three components of income, rather than money alone, is significant. Ideally, the marriage team tries to make decisions that result in a balance of the three.

The three components of income all involve money in one way or another. This means that savings in each of the marriage periods fortify the succeeding stage and reach the climax of their importance in the last period.

Saving for the future is a matter of building resources for all kinds of income. For non-dollar income this means developing and conserving the resources of knowledge and know-how, education, and strength and energy. It also means developing and conserving resources that will reduce dollar income requirements. High among these resources is home ownership. It is true that owning one's home, even if it is fully paid for, does not eliminate the cost of shelter. There are always taxes and costs of upkeep and repair for the homeowner to pay. However, non-dollar income resources, including equipment, can cut the maintenance costs. So home ownership may be counted as a form of savings. It is also an asset that can be turned into cash in an emergency.

Future dollar income, when wages or salaries no longer contribute or are inadequate, comes from the resource of money itself in the form of investments—not an accumulated collection of dollars waiting to be spent. Even the dollar income provided by Social Security or retirement plans comes from investment. The availability of dollar income in the future depends on setting aside small amounts of money from time to time in order to accumulate enough dollars to constitute income-paying investments rather than a stock of cash, which forty years from now may not be worth what it is now. This is the basis for Social Security withholding amounts, and other pay deductions. Actually, the dollars paid into Social Security or other retirement plans are a kind of enforced budgeting, but the process of budgeting is much more involved.

A basic guideline to budgeting is that what works for one marriage team may not work for another, especially where interrelationships are involved. A rigidly enforced budget can be just as disastrous to husband-wife relationships as no budget at all can be to economic security. Two people seldom entirely agree, emotionally, on the relative value of different items that make up the three aspects of income. For this reason the team approach, with plenty of discussion and give and take, is much better than the authoritarian individual approach.

The first budgets of the young marriage team should be experimental, to prove whether or not they are both economically and emotionally trustworthy. This implies very careful record-keeping. Periodically, the team should go over the records carefully and make decisions about budget adjustments, always keeping in mind that there are three aspects of income and two aspects of budgeting—one short-range and the other long-range.

In planning even an experimental budget, you should be aware of some of the problems that can arise. For example, "sample budgets" that have been tested by experts against costs of living are useful in suggesting how general proportions of dollar income may be allocated, but what worked well five years ago may no longer be a useful guide.

Probably the most common money management problem results from what is called the "upside-down budget." The "rightside-up budget" begins by allocating portions of the dollar income to necessities like clothing, food, shelter, and provisions for the future. Then, if there's any money left over, it's tabbed for less essential items, non-essential items, or luxuries. The upside-down budget starts with these and assigns the left-over income to the essentials.

One financial counselor admits that some luxuries may be psychological necessities and suggests that the solution is to list these first in the budget, remembering that the remainder of the income has to be parceled out among the items such as food, clothing, shelter, heat, and so forth. In other words, if a color television set is actually a necessity, you may have to eat macaroni and cheese instead of roast beef. This way of thinking, however, can be a budget trap. The bait is partly advertising and partly the illuson that "other people manage somehow, even though they don't make any more money than we do." Maybe this is true, but if it is, the chances are that they are eating macaroni and cheese too. The roast-beef eaters usually have rightside-up budgets.

There are other traps hidden along the path of money management. One is "the easy credit trap." This one can break your financial back in a hurry—and, of course, completely nullify the most carefully constructed rightside-up budget. It is fairly easy to spot this trap, but sometimes it is difficult to resist the bait even when you know the trap is underneath. When someone offers to sell you an electric refrigerator, for instance, with "instant credit"—nothing down and no payment until some (apparently) distant future date—there's something fishy. How much are the payments going to be when they do begin? How many of them will there be? Is there a high "carrying charge" that amounts to more than the interest you would pay if you borrowed the purchase money from a bank?

Perhaps the stated price of the refrigerator is considerably less than the standard list price, but if it is, there has to be a reason.

One may be legitimate: the dealer simply accepts a smaller profit. But more frequently he may be making more out of the carrying charge than on the sale of the refrigerator. Another gimmick is to stretch the payments over so long a time that the refrigerator may wear out or need expensive repair before you have finished paying for it.

A neat way to avoid this trap is to accept the standard list price or legitimate discount price (not a sale price), and then make the same monthly payments the dealer proposed *to yourself* in a bank savings account, which pays you interest. Then you can pay cash for the refrigerator. Of course, you will have to wait, but it's usually worthwhile.

Another financial trap is "imaginary money." It is only natural to think of income as the amount of dollars per hour, per week, per month that you are paid by your employer or some other source. It is easy to forget the withholding taxes and other taxes that are inescapable, whether paid directly or indirectly. These amounts have to be deducted from dollar income rather than regarded as expenditures.

Also, you may imagine that income at any particular moment will be the same or higher at a future time. Unless there is real assurance of continued employment or advancement, it is easy to make a mistake about dollar income next year when it is figured on the basis of dollar income this year.

Still another aspect of the "imaginary money" trap is the buying power of the dollar. Remember that money has meaning only in terms of goods and services. A dollar won't buy as many goods and services now as it would ten years ago, and it seems that every succeeding year it buys fewer and fewer goods and services, thus raising "the cost of living." This is why so many labor unions have insisted upon an automatic cost-of-living increase in standard wages. If your dollar income is not regulated by this automatic device, you may discover that a considerable portion of it is imaginary in practical terms of the goods and services it will buy.

The trap of "forgotten items" is one you may set for yourself, by not keeping complete and accurate records of expenditures so that you have something on which to base your short-term budgeting. For instance, if you forget that an annual insurance premium is due June 15, your June budget will be upset.

In making up any budget, it is easy to forget little items that nonetheless mount up. You may remember "utilities" but forget the water bill. You budget gasoline for the car, probably, but do you remember the cost of an oil change every thirty days or one-thousand miles? You remember Christmas presents, but what about wrapping paper? The list is interminable, and there's no need to itemize everything. You can make a check-up analysis every once in a while and strike a monthly average.

Then there is another category of forgotten items—the ones you forget because if you have been lucky you have not had much experience with them. These are things like major automobile repairs, sudden failure of the hot-water heater, or the need to paint the house or the bathroom. You can't always budget for these specifically; but if you don't allow margins for them you may find you simply can't take care of them when they drop on you without warning.

It would be a mistake to leave the topic of money management without discussing credit in general. Your credit is your reputation for being a safe person to lend money to. But your reputation for being a good "loan risk" is not based on rumor or some vague impression that you can be trusted. It is based on the carefully kept records of banks from which you have borrowed money and businesses that have allowed you to buy things and charge them. If you pay what you owe promptly when due, along with interest or carrying charges, you can get the next loan or make the next purchase on time a great deal more easily.

The records of your loan and charge payments are not just filed away with the individual bank or business involved. These records are either pooled in a credit bureau or are available to any other bank or business from which you want to borrow or buy. The first bank loan you get is the most difficult. The first loan will be made on the basis of recommendations from people who know you personally (and who may be asked to take responsibility for the loan if you fail to pay it back), your stated and proved dollar income, and the way the bank sizes you up. If you handle that first loan promptly, the next one, or loans from other banks or loan companies, may be a little larger than the first, because you have begun to establish a good credit rating. This is a definite resource for dollar income as well as an asset.

You will have a poor credit rating if you don't pay promptly, and this will make loans harder to get. Furthermore, no credit rating at all can be just as embarrassing as a poor one. Some young people have found it necessary to borrow money they didn't need and pay the same money back, just to establish their credit. The only cost was the interest. This practice is recommended only if the temptation to use the money impulsively for an unplanned purchase can be avoided.

The use of dollar income by a marriage team is a vast and complicated subject. It may appear that getting the income and learning how to use it will dominate your married life, but it really doesn't. You will have quite a lot of leisure time, and how you use it is just as important as how you use your income.

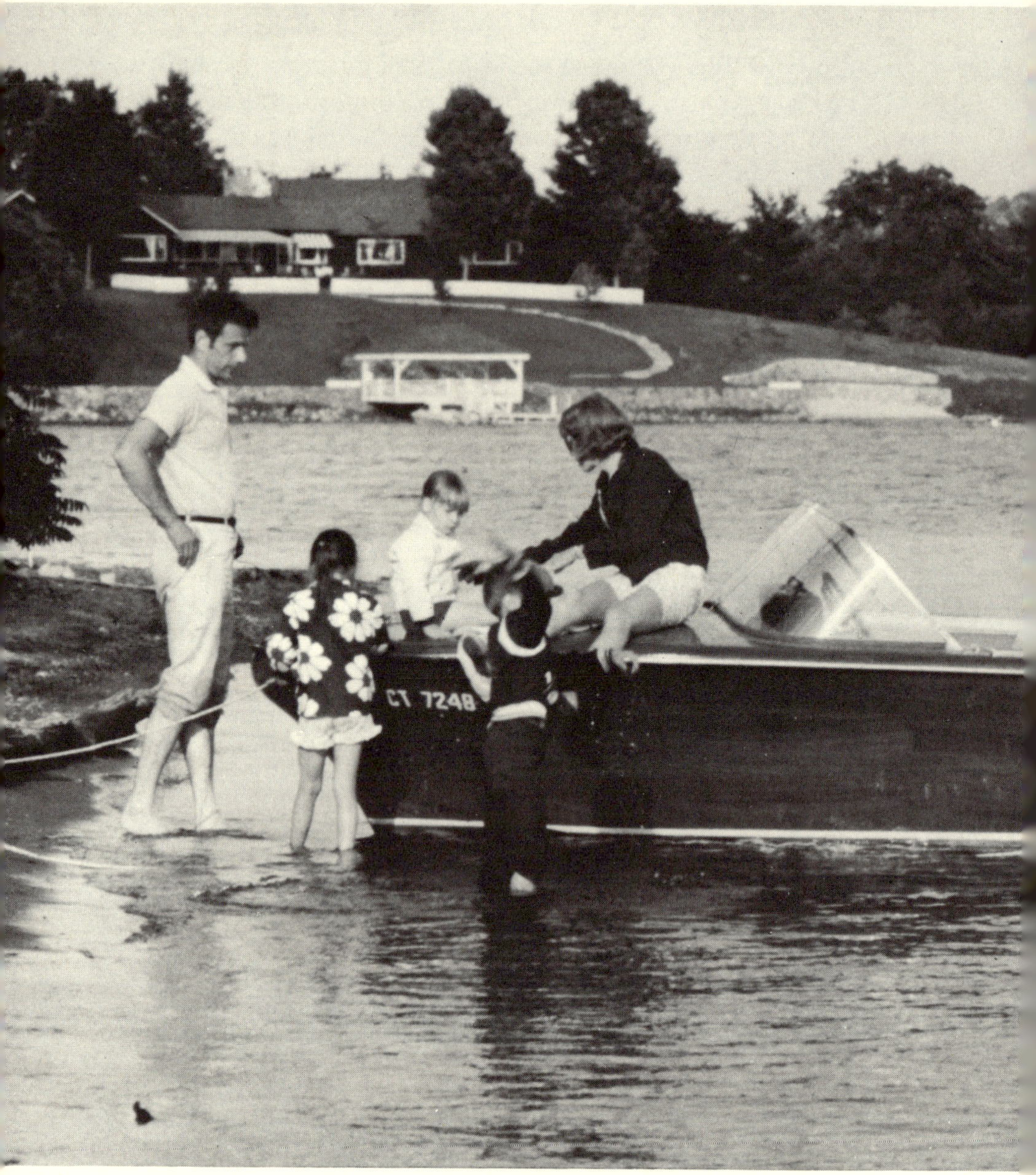
CT 7248

7

Leisure Time

> This time, like all times, is a very good one
> If we know what to do with it.
> —RALPH WALDO EMERSON

The importance of marriage team decisions about the use of leisure time is often overlooked, because leisure time use may overlap so many other areas that it loses its identity. Decisions about money, friends, family, and other matters frequently involve decisions about use of leisure time, even though the connection is not obvious at the time the team makes the decisions.

Defining or explaining leisure time is not quite as simple as you might think. In general, you can think of leisure time as "off-the-job time." First, though, you must consider what "the job" is. Primarily, of course, it is the production of both dollar and non-dollar income. But not all of the household tasks in marriage can be classified as non-dollar income producers, because they don't always offer a really valid choice between hiring them done and doing them yourself. Shopping, keeping accounts, paying bills, keeping house, and practically everything that goes into bringing up children are parts of the job in marriage for the vast majority of people. Taking the baby for a stroll in the park is part of the job of being a parent, especially for mothers. Being a Little League baseball fan may be another parental job, especially for fathers. Even being an active member of the PTA is part of the job of parenthood.

Take all the time used in doing things like these, and add it to the time used in producing dollar income, as well as the time spent for such necessities as eating, sleeping, and brushing teeth. Subtract this, on a weekly, monthly, or yearly basis, from all the hours there are, and what's left over is leisure time. This leisure time is, in a sense, earned by each of the two individual members of the marriage team. The situation, then, is very much like that in which both partners produce dollar income. The same basic questions must be answered: "Whose leisure time is it? Is it mine, yours, or ours?"

Decisions about the answer to this question are frequently more difficult to make than when dollar income is the question. Occasionally it is possible for a married couple to pool leisure time, but for the most part, leisure time has to be used when it is available. You can seek a joint two-week vacation, perhaps, but, if both husband and wife are wage earners their vacations may not coincide.

Aside from vacations, the daily or weekly ration of leisure time is likely to be different when husband and wife are both employed. About 30 per cent of all workers in the United States now work at some time other than the daylight hours. If either you or your husband or wife are part of this 30 per cent, your leisure times won't coincide.

Another situation presents a problem in planned leisure time use. In many jobs, the days off shift from week to week and often not in accordance with any pre-arranged schedule. What use of leisure time would be adaptable to this situation? Right along with this go the variations in peak loads of work in some occupations. For instance, steelworkers usually have more leisure around Christmas than at any other time of the year. On the other hand, people connected with retail sales have less leisure at this time of the year.

The same kind of situation, in a different sense, applies when the wife is not a dollar income producer. Her leisure times are likely to match her husband's leisure times only in part, at the best. She is cooking supper when her husband comes home from work. After supper she clears the table and washes the dishes. If the husband helps with these jobs, the time isn't leisure time for either, although it does have potential value for both in terms of later leisure and immediate interrelationships. But the leisure time of the non-working wife is, typically, when her husband is buried in non-leisure activity at work and her children are in school or at rest. Therefore, the answer to the question, "Whose leisure time is it?" usually falls in two parts. Part of the combined leisure time is ours; but each of us has a portion of personal leisure to use in any way we want.

The team process, however, still operates. The team makes decisions concerned with the jointly owned leisure time, and it also makes decisions about the use of individual leisure time. In this way each member of the team can benefit by the thinking of the other, and they can avoid the dangerous split in ideas about leisure that has wrecked many a marriage. In making these decisions, the team can take a number of considerations into account.

The amount of available leisure time for the team, jointly and separately, depends on the production of both dollar and non-dollar income and how both are used. For instance, double-jobbing cuts deeply into leisure time, but double-jobbing may be—or appear to be—absolutely essential. Frequently, the necessity is based on unwise use of dollar income rather than on an inadequate amount of it. The team's decision, then, involves weighing the values of leisure time against the possible ways of making double-jobbing unnecessary.

The production of non-dollar income also affects the supply of leisure time, especially for wives. Some home economists have said for quite a while that women can use as much as twice the time they need in housekeeping, thus cutting into their leisure time. The following story illustrates this point.

In Minneapolis recently a schoolteacher . . . read a story in the local newspaper about the long work week of today's housewife. Declaring in a letter to the editor

> that "any woman who puts in that many hours is awfully slow, a poor budgeter of time, or just plain inefficient," this thirty-six-year-old bachelor offered to take over any household and show how it could be done.
>
> Scores of irate housewives dared him to prove it. He took over [a] household . . . with four children, aged two to seven, for three days. In a single day, he cleaned the first floor, washed three loads of clothes and hung them out to dry, ironed all the laundry including underwear and sheets, fixed a soup-and-sandwich lunch and a big backyard supper, baked two cakes, prepared two salads for the next day, dressed, undressed, and bathed the children, washed woodwork and scrubbed the kitchen floor.[8]

Of course, we don't know anything about the quality of the man's work, but he showed that the home economists may be right.

Another aspect of the economics of leisure is the dollar cost of leisure time use. Many possible uses of leisure time cost money—sometimes quite a lot of it. Hence, it is easy to see that you could have an upside-down budget with use of leisure at the top as a luxury. This might result, for instance, from spending a lot of your leisure time in a bar, or from devoting most of your leisure time to playing golf at an expensive club. For that matter, playing golf anywhere is an expensive way of using leisure, even though it may be justified by some of its satisfactions.

Decisions about use of leisure time must be made in the same spirit and in much the same way you make decisions about purchasing goods and services. Costs have to be weighed against values. You can think of these values in terms of income if you begin by regarding leisure time as a resource. What are some of the income items derived from this resource if it is developed and used?

As the amount of leisure time increases, the importance of work declines, and there is more and more need for personal identity and more opportunity to establish it through the use of leisure time. In an earlier chapter we had a look at Martha Jones, who was "just a housewife" serving on a citizens' committee. By using her leisure time to serve on that committee, she was establishing an identity quite apart from her position as "housewife."

When work, in the sense of producing dollar and non-dollar income, dominated man's life and occupied the major part of his waking hours, identity for both men and women came from the kind of work they did. Now it can come from the use of leisure time.

Suppose a shoe-salesman in his leisure time becomes a rockhound. Rockhounding involves seeking out rare and semiprecious stones and rocks, plus cutting and polishing them to reveal their beauty. Sometimes it includes collecting fossils, too. It calls for a good deal of knowledge about where to look for what kind of stone or rock, and the ability to identify and name what is found. It also requires special skill in polishing. All in all, although it seldom produces any dollar income, rockhounding conveys more status than shoeselling. Except for dollar income purposes, this man would rather be identified as a rockhound than as a salesman, because it proves that he is something of a geologist, a bit of a mineralogist, and has some of the skills of a lapidary.

Now, suppose the salesman was elected president of the Rockhounds of Ziltchville. This would involve an obligation and a lot of energy and brain-use. It would not be a hobby and it would certainly not be recreation, but it would give him another kind of personal identity and status. Maybe this particular role wouldn't be valuable to everyone, but if it is for the salesman, it is a good use of his leisure time—provided it does not bring him into conflict with his wife and children.

You don't have to be elected president of an organization to benefit from its identity. Just being a member can do the same thing, provided membership is active. This is one of the reasons all sorts of civic clubs, professional associations, and community-action councils flourish.

Possibly this identity value is just a shade more important for women than for men, because, in our culture, women are apt to blend their personal and individual identity with that of their husbands. In other words, through marriage, women may tend to lose some personal identity, which they can renew by using some non-work time in active participation in an organization.

Establishment of a sense of identity is not a selfish matter. It does not isolate the individual or make him self-centered. On the contrary, the feeling of personal worth, of being something more than a Social Security number with an occupation, is a necessity for happy relationships with other people, includng the marriage partner.

Another income value of leisure time is its potential for rest and relaxation. This value is primarily individual, but it can be enjoyed by husband and wife together. The idea, of course, is that some portion of the time not spent in earning a living is used to recover the energy and strength expended on the job and to escape the humdrum of daily work. This is a very sensitive and dangerous area for either the individual or the team, because it is easy to go to extremes.

Some people seem to have inherited a feeling of guilt about not being "busy." The Puritans warned strongly against the dangers of idleness and saw the Devil at work whenever a person really relaxed. A lot of people today who are not worried about the Devil still avoid relaxation because they think of it as idleness. With more available leisure time than the Puritans had, many people jump from the deadly grind of income producing to an equally deadly grind in another activity. They may not really leave the grind at all. Some men, especially, are always on the job, thinking and worrying about it and probably dreaming about it, even when they aren't at work. Quite a few of these men "enjoy" ulcers instead of leisure.

Rest and relaxation may include recreation, which of course, can include vigorous activities like skiing, playing tennis, or hiking. But even these forms of recreation can be restful in that they offer a change from the usual pattern of activity. For the desk-worker, a tough mountain climb may actually be very relaxing.

Recreation is not always active, and, whether it is or not, its chief contribution to the value of rest and relaxation is change of pace and escape from boredom. It is natural to become bored with your job once in a while, and to use recreation to escape from it. If you are bored when you are *not* on the job, you don't need recreation; you need more of the other values that leisure time can provide.

Personal growth and development is a leisure time dividend that complements personal identity and overlaps it to some extent. Part of it involves creativity, which is the satisfaction of a basic human need for self-expression by actually creating something that did not exist before. The value of the item created is not of much importance as long as the individual has the satisfaction of making something with his own hands, his own mind, and his own imagination.

There is a kind of vicarious creativity in learning to recognize and get pleasure and stimulation from the creativity of others. Without being able to play a note on any musical instrument, you may still satisfy some of your creative needs by learning to appreciate the patterns and intricacies of a symphony. This is one of the most valid of all uses of leisure time, and fortunately it is easily available nowadays if you have a television set. Watching "educational TV" programs is a leisure time activity with double value. It offers creative satisfaction along with husband-wife companionship.

Companionship has become perhaps the most important reward of modern marriage. Studies have shown that women are likely to rate it above love, children, or economic security. Husbands have not been so thoroughly canvassed, but there is no reason to doubt that they, too, place companionship high on the scale of the rewards of marriage.

In marriage today, companionship can mostly be achieved only in leisure time. This is why it has become so important and why the emphasis on it is a social phenomenon. In early America, husband and wife found companionship through work in the field or shop. Sometimes modern couples can achieve this. (For instance, one man and his wife ran what they called a "Mama and Papa grocery store." They wanted to keep it that way because they consciously valued the companionship it offered, but business got too good. They had to hire extra help and lost some of the companionship.)

But the overwhelming majority of American couples can expect little companionship in the production of dollar income. They may achieve some by sharing parts of the non-dollar income work, but companionship is chiefly a product of leisure time.

The emphasis on companionship in marriage has resulted in a new word in the American language—*togetherness*. This was once a pretty good word for expressing the companionship described here, but it has lost its original force. Some people have tried to make almost a religion out of togetherness, without realizing that it does not automatically provide companionship. Making a fetish of togetherness in marriage may lead people to forget that the value of companionship is not restricted to husband-wife relationships. It extends to the companionship of a husband with other men, a wife with other women, and the couple with other couples.

There is also something to be said in favor of "separateness." Perhaps husbands are slightly more apt than wives to feel the need for this value. Men today are likely to find themselves in a female-oriented world, especially in view of the increasing number of working women in practically all fields. Perhaps togetherness with their wives may occasionally seem to be the final straw for some men.

Many wives who do not work outside the home may have ample opportunity for same-sex relationships, if only in neighborhood kaffee klatsches, and some of these relationships may develop into companionship. The employed wife does not have as much opportunity for same-sex companionship, even if she works in a female-dominated office. There isn't time in a ten-minute coffee-break for much companionship. She will have to find it elsewhere, in leisure time. For both husbands and wives, clubs and organizations of various sorts may fill the bill. Team decisions about leisure time should take this into account.

There are several other bases for marriage team decisions regarding use of leisure time.

Despite the fact that we all have more leisure time today than our grandparents had, it is still limited, and unlike other resources, it cannot be replenished. Moreover, there is no substitute for leisure time. It is not like non-dollar income, which is a substitute for dollar income. You can't borrow it from a bank, like dollars, or manipulate it by double-jobbing. You have a fixed amount of leisure time, and what you use for one purpose can't be used for another.

The possible values of leisure time use are like the values in various kinds of food—carbohydrates, proteins, minerals, and vitamins. If you get too much of any one of these, you will likely miss some of the others. In marriage the same principle applies to the values of leisure time use for both members of the team, individually and together. You need a balanced diet of leisure time values. Sometimes it is difficult to provide that diet because of another factor.

For the individual and for the couple there is nothing else in marriage quite so habit-forming as the use of leisure time, and no other factor in marriage, not even dollar income, is so closely tied to the stages of married life.

Use of leisure time tends to fall into a pattern, or a set of patterns. The patterns formed in the period of establishment may either have to be abandoned or adjusted (sometimes with difficulty and a painful wrench) in the expanding-family period. Child-care comes under the heading of "on-the-job-time," so in the period of the expanding family there will automatically be less leisure time for both husband and wife than in the first stage. It seems reasonable, then, to suggest that decisions about the use of leisure time should take into account the changes that may have to be made when children are involved.

Your children are apt to acquire the same general habits of leisure time use that you and your marriage partner have, or reflect some of the results of your choice. This does not mean that just because you play bridge or poker in your leisure time your children will do the same thing. Of course they might, but the important thing to think about here is the general pattern. It has been shown over and over that children who have difficulty with reading and writing in school are apt to have parents who don't use much of their leisure time in reading. Although this is not an absolute rule, it has been shown to be true frequently enough to offer a hint, and it reflects parental use of leisure time.

When you reach the retirement period, the habitual patterns of leisure time count even more—only sometimes in a backhanded way. One professional man said frankly that he did not dare retire, although he was eligible, because he had never learned how to use his leisure. He felt that with no interests other than his work, he would die within a few years at the most. Actually, this does happen more frequently than you might suppose.

These are the basic values, and some considerations, to be taken into account when the marriage team makes decisions and sets policies about leisure time. When you come to apply these considerations and values to specific activities or general areas of activities, you discover a great deal of overlapping of values and many problems in weighing one consideration against another. High on the list of necessary considerations is the matter of total family relationships.

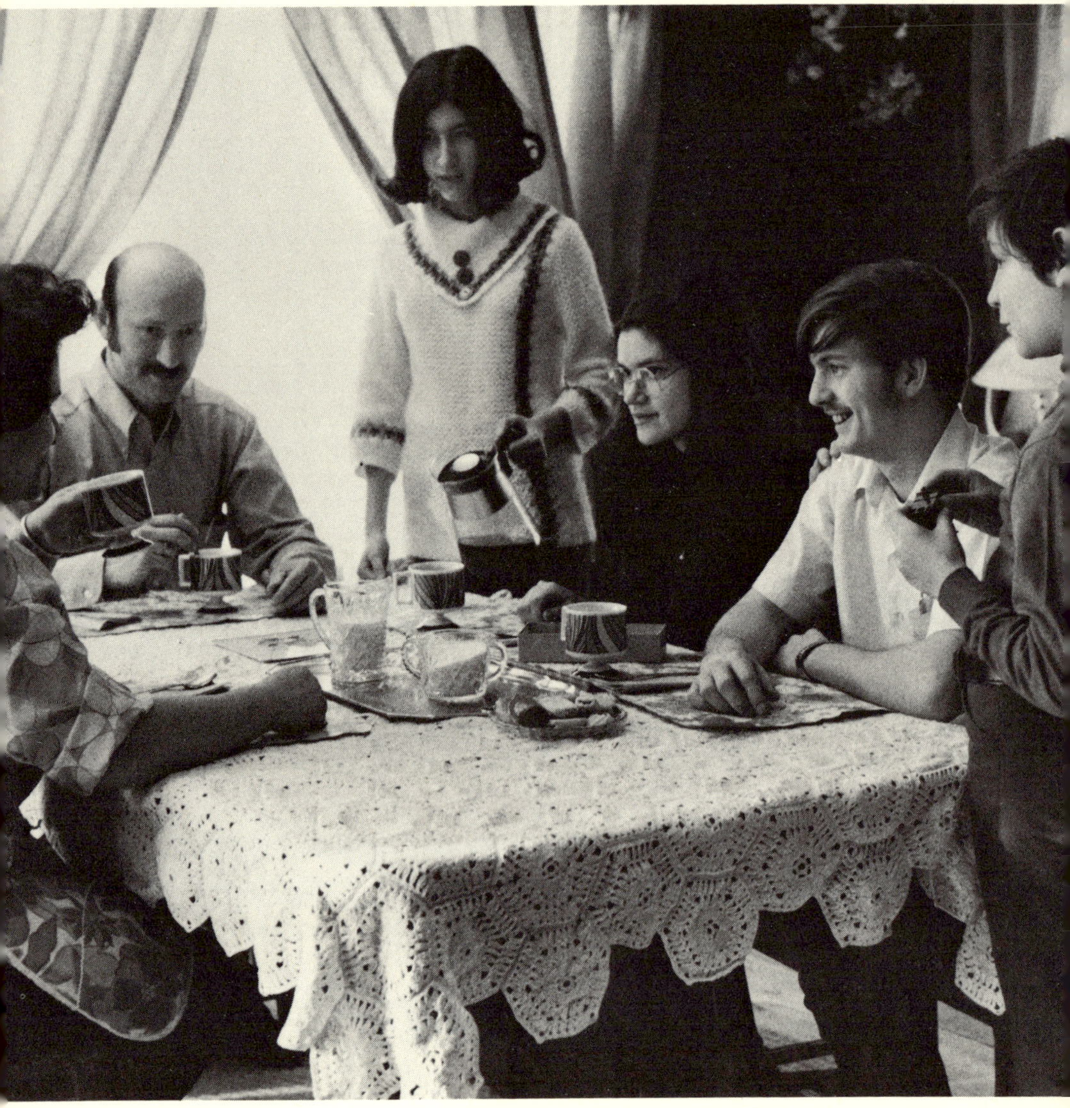

8

Family and Family Roles

Mon enfant! I give you my hand!
I give you my love, more precious than money,
I give you myself, before preaching or law;
Will you give me yourself? Will you come travel with me?
Shall we stick by each other as long as we live?
—WALT WHITMAN: "Song of the Open Road"

Social scientists have studied the family in all its forms and complexities. They have found that ideas about the family profoundly influence modern marriage because these ideas are so likely to be based on divergent backgrounds and unconscious learning of attitudes. Social scientists have also worked out a vocabulary which makes it possible to talk about family in universal terms. They have used this vocabulary in reporting what they have learned, specifically, about the influence of family on marriage, and the problems created by divergent ideas.

In social science terminology, there are two basic types of family: *nuclear* and *extended*. A nuclear family is a husband and wife and all their dependent children. It is called a nuclear family because it is the nucleus of still other families formed when the dependent children become independent, get married, and have children of their own. You came from a nuclear family and so did your marriage partner.

Nuclear families are of two sorts. The nuclear family in which you grew up is called your family of orientation. After you are married and presumably have children, the nuclear family in which you occupy the position of husband or wife is called the family of procreation. In other words, you, your spouse and your children (until they are married) compose a family of procreation. Both of these are nuclear families, but the two different terms suggest different functions and attitudes related to the nuclear family.

To explain what is meant by the *extended family*, we need to introduce still another social science term—kinfolk (or sometimes kin or kinsmen). Kinfolk are people who share a common ancestor. Your sisters and brothers are kinfolk because you and they have the same parents. Your uncles and aunts are kinfolk because you share with them a common ancestor in the person of your grandfather or grandmother, who is their father or mother. The children of your aunts and uncles are your cousins, and the children of your brothers and sisters are your nieces and nephews. When you have children, they will be cousins of your nieces and nephews. All of these are kinfolk, even though you may not have met some of them. And whether or not any of them, including yourself, are adopted does not affect the relationship in any way.

Your partner's kinfolk are not technically yours. You do not normally share a common ancestor, although there are families where husband and wife do have an ancestor in common somewhere in the past, particularly in instances where prestige and wealth are important and maintained from generation to generation. For most people, however, the marriage partner's kinfolk are "in-law" kinfolk, because marriage is a legal contract establishing a relationship between each partner in the family of the other partner. For practical purposes, all the kinfolk of both you and your partner can be grouped together in defining the extended family. In the sociologist's vocabulary, your marriage partner's family is called your family of affinal relations.

From the social science point of view, then, the extended family is made up of the two families of orientation, the family of procreation, and the family of affinal relations. In simpler terms, your extended family consists of you and your marriage partner, plus all the kinfolk of both you and your spouse. Your children, when you have them, will join the extended family group with various designations ranging from grandson or granddaughter, to niece or nephew and cousin, with appropriate affinal relationships in the same categories. All the "in-law" connections are involved.

You can see that this could result in a very complicated and intricate network involving a great many nuclear families, as it does in some cultures. The traditional Chinese family, for instance; is a classical illustration. In this system there might be a dozen nuclear families, all held together by father-son relationships and perhaps living together in a collection of more or less connected houses in what is called a compound. If there was another compound, it was usually within the same small village.

The American extended family is usually thought of as consisting of only two interlocking groups of persons: the parents and brothers and sisters of both marriage partners. For the most part, we are chiefly concerned with parents, grandparents, sisters and brothers, aunts and uncles—both blood and in-law.

Actually, from the genealogical point of view, children of brothers and sisters are also members of the extended family. In some societies, and for some families, cousins are extremely important in the family structure. And even their children (second cousins) may also be important. All this depends upon the relationships of the original members of the family of orientation and the following families of procreation. These relationships depend on basic ideas about what some sociologists call *familism* and *nonfamilism.*

One writer explains familism this way: "In the familistic setting, one interacts with one's kinsmen because they are kinsmen. If in addition to being related to them, one also likes them, so much the better; if not, so much the worse, but the latter attitude does not lead to social withdrawal." [9]

Nonfamilism is, as you might guess, the exact reverse of this attitude. In a nonfamilistic setting, if one does not like one's kinsmen or kinfolk, one does withdraw from them socially. As a matter of fact, some people feel so strongly about nonfamilism that it sometimes appears they withdraw from kinsmen simply because they are kinsmen and not necessarily because they don't like them. Familism and nonfamilism stand for bedrock ways of thinking about, or automatically accepting, a way of life. Of course we have noted only the two extremes of familism and nonfamilism. In between, there are almost infinite degrees of devotion to one or the other of the two ideas.

For a long time sociologists considered that nonfamilism was the normative attitude of the American family system. Married couples were advised to stay as far away as possible from their families of orientation. This teaching probably accounts for some of the "in-law problems" and also for many other problems of relationship between husbands and wives that were, and still are, frequently very potent.

The isolated nuclear family is simply the family of procreation, theoretically as nearly as possible independent of the extended family. The pioneer family sketched by Margaret Mead's description in Chapter 3 is a perfect illustration of the simon-pure version of this kind of family. Here the husband and wife and their children were isolated from their extended families by both geographical and emotional distance. They were strictly on their own.

Some sociologists believe that this kind of family became the standard American pattern because it was the only kind of family which could meet the peculiar requirements of American life. It provided freedom of movement from one place to another, unhampered by ties with extended families, and it freed Americans from the restrictions of class, religion, traditional occupations and other identification with extended families.

The isolated nuclear family is based on the ability of husband and wife to be both independent and self-sufficient, because they had to be this way in order to survive. It remained the standard marriage and family pattern even when the necessity for independence was no longer strongly felt. Writers of books on marriage, until a few years ago, frequently stated that continued close relationships with families of orientation was a sign of emotional immaturity.

Today, when you set up your own nuclear family, you will not be able to keep isolated from the rest of the extended family whether you want to or not. It is too easy for other family members to call you, to pull up in front of your house, or to come to town unexpectedly. And of course you can do the same thing with them when you feel the need for a visit or assistance. The important point is that the American nuclear family was probably never as isolated as it was reported. Actually the American family system provides many of the advantages of the extended family, and at the same time provides opportunity for the advantages of the isolated family. It is a sort of a compromise system, which has not been formally recognized and described, although many sociologists have been observing its development and growth.

The new American family idea does not change the concept of the American marriage team and its functioning. Instead it gives the partners in the marriage team more to work with in making their decisions and setting their policies than they would have if they were completely isolated. All the members of the extended family can be counted as resources in the same way that the couple has resources for income. One decision the marriage team has to make is whether or not they will avail themselves of these resources.

The theory of the isolated nuclear family would prevent this use of resources, at least to a degree. But if the isolated nuclear family is more "fiction than fact," you are free to make a choice. It will cost you something to develop this resource, because while members of the extended family have a great deal to offer, they can also demand a great deal. If you allow them to, they can disturb your leisure time budget, and it is possible that they may upset your dollar and nondollar budget too. Most important is the need to understand and to interact satisfactorily and happily with the extended family. This leads inevitably to the same sort of question asked in the last two chapters. "Whose extended family is it? Is it yours, mine, or ours?"

A married woman usually takes the family name of her husband. There are some families who regard the family name of the wife as so important that they hyphenate the name of the family of procreation. (For example: Pierce-Jones.)

In some countries and cultures, the mother's family name is used or adopted when the daughter marries, but this practice is rather uncommon, especially in modern life; but it does reflect an influence of familism versus nonfamilism that affects many people, even though they do not show it in the extreme way of combining family names. However, feelings and attitudes toward in-laws and other extended family members are not automatically negative, even in the very beginning, and they may not involve much adjustment in later years. There is a good deal of evidence to show that many marriages are based on the liking of each partner for the prospective in-laws and other extended family members of the other partner.

Sociologists who have studied the way American families of procreation line up with respect to their emphasis on one family of orientation or the other are not entirely agreed in their findings and conclusions. One writer says: "Every investigation of kinship ties in the United States has shown that mother-daughter associations constitute the core around which most contacts with relatives are organized." [10] The same writer finds some differences in the pattern based on socio-economic class, but not many.

You can easily see why this question has to be discussed and settled if the expectations of one member of the marriage team are in one direction and the desires of the other in another direction. Observation and study of the subject from several different points of view indicate that there is a good deal of practical truth in the old poem: "My son's my son till he gets him a wife, but my daughter's my daughter all her life." It is probably especially important that husbands understand this tendency of wives and their parents. Sometimes the husband may see in his wife's close association with her parents a fancied indication of lack of love or loyalty to him. On top of this, the stereotype of the mother-in-law from the husband's point of view is well fixed by a tremendous collection of mother-in-law jokes and cartoons.

The truth is that there are very likely to be sex-based differences in attitudes toward families of orientation. For a number of reasons, wives are more likely than husbands to be "family conscious."

Parents tend to treat sons differently from the way they treat daughters. They give boys a great deal more freedom and a lot more privacy than they give daughters. By and large, most parents push their sons toward independence as fast as they can, whereas they try to keep daughters dependent as long as possible. Of course, this is not a universal law, it is merely an observation of the general situation to which there are a great many individual exceptions. "Daughter protection" is a habit in most families, and it is not easily and simply broken just because the daughter gets married.

Sometimes mothers, especially, try to do the same sort of protective job for their sons, and occasionally the son lets her get away with it. Usually, however, sons get untangled from the mother's apron strings as soon as possible, sometimes even before adolescence. Fathers usually help sons untie the apron-string knots, while at the same time they tie more of them for daughter. Like all generalizations about social phenomena, this one is subject to a great many variations and exceptions; but it is valid enough to warrant a good deal of thought.

When women get married, they may be led to attempt playing two different and conflicting sets of roles—those connected with the position of wife and those associated with the position of daughter. If the wife recognizes that actually she is now in the position of married daughter rather than daughter, and can work out a satisfactory accompanying role for this new set of relationships, things are likely to go more smoothly. Husbands are not likely to experience this kind of role conflict as often as their wives, but sometimes they do.

The differences members of the marriage team have concerning the extended family depend a great deal upon the age of the husband and wife.

The common phrase "adolescent revolt" is often used to describe a normal part of everyone's development. Adolescent revolt is the result of both the social and biological pressure to become independent of parents and other people who have been supervising and protecting the young person from earliest infancy to the time he feels himself old enough and strong enough to "be his own boss."

This feeling of revolt can be very strong, and the expression of the feeling rather violent. Probably all of you have felt at some time or other that you really hated, or at least disliked, your parents, your older brothers or sisters, or anyone else in the family who tried to tell you what to do and how to do it. This period of revolt can last a long time. Most people outgrow it, but some don't. Failure to outgrow these feelings results either from the failure of the people who are being revolted against to understand the situation or, more frequently, from the rebel's going so far in adolescent revolt that there is no retreat. You become committed to something you can't escape.

In the trend toward early marriage, many social scientists and counselors see the possibility that some young people may find marriage a means of expressing their feeling of revolt against family authority and domination. Even if the marriage is not actually part of the revolt, there may be some feelings associated with that stage of development that make interactions with extended family members more difficult. Research shows that the lower the age of the marriage partners, the more likely they are to have both in-law and other extended family problems. Of course this is not always the situation in every early marriage, but it is important to realize that when any marriage, regardless of the age of the couple, is used as a way of escaping from the family, the valuable resources available from the extended family are likely to be cut off.

There are some other effects of the age of the marriage team members on their relationships and interactions with the extended family. The younger you are when you get married, the more likely you are to need the financial support and other forms of help from members of the extended family. This is especially true if you plan to continue your education after marriage. Imagine a young husband and wife arguing about almost any decision, and the husband saying, "Gee, honey, we just can't do that, because Dad wouldn't like it and he'd cut off our allowance." It doesn't seem necessary to analyze further that situation and its affect on the future of the marriage involved.

Extended family relationships can be almost as changeable as the weather. If you wait a few years, your feelings about members of the extended family, and their feelings about you, can change providing you can keep negative feelings from becoming fixed and also develop and continue the positive, or good, feelings. This involves some conscious and perhaps difficult personal adjustments.

Everything we know about in-law problems and extended family relationships and interaction boils down to a central idea—*acceptance*.

Perhaps when you first started high school you had quite a few friends who came along with you from your previous school. But you were in a new school building, a new environment, and there were a lot of new ways of doing things, rules that were not actually written down but were understood by the oldtimers in the higher classes. They looked at you as you walked down the hall, and you knew that they spotted you as a freshman without any difficulty. After a while, however, some of these exhalted upperclassmen began to recognize you in the hall and perhaps even call you by name and ask for a favor. You began to feel you were accepted as a high-school student.

Something of the same sort happens in marriage. Feeling accepted by your marriage partner's kinfolk is likely to be a very important factor in your married life. These kinfolk whose acceptance you would like to have, however, are people just as you are, and they have all the little twists and quirks that make people human. All people have feelings which can be hurt, and all are perfectly capable of hurting the feelings of others. People have likes and dislikes and prejudices concerning many things, including some other people. Although your feeling of being accepted is important, it is also important that you give the kinfolk the idea that you accept them also.

There are some fairly common situations that make both of these acceptances a little difficult at the very beginning of marriage. A lot of these circumstances originated in the period when you and your husband or wife were dating.

If you are the new husband, the chances are good that your wife's parents, and perhaps other kinfolk, have had more opportunity to get acquainted with you than your parents and kinfolk have had to be acquainted with your wife. If you followed the usual dating practice before marriage, you called for your date at her home and gave her kinfolk (if she was living with them) the chance to have a look at you and form certain impressions. On the other hand, a lot of brides never see their husband's kinfolk until shortly before the wedding. Everybody on the groom's side of the team, therefore, has to start from scratch in learning acceptance. From the other point of view, the bride's kinfolk may have decided against acceptance of the husband long before he became an in-law.

The studies that sociologists have made of marriages with in-law problems, and happy and successful marriages in general, show that acceptance and approval of bride and groom by both sets of kinfolk before marriage is one of the most significant factors in developing the marriage itself. It is particularly important because before marriage each person is accepted simply as himself or herself. But there are other aspects of acceptance.

Everyone in the family is assigned a new societal position when you get married. Everybody becomes an in-law to somebody else, and some of the people involved may not take kindly to the idea of accepting the new position and the roles and complementary roles called for. As far as you are concerned, you can probably learn to accept your new position and role, if you put your mind to it and really try, but what are you going to do about the others?

The people involved in extended families can be almost as important to your marriage as you and your marriage partner are. But other people can be influenced and given the understanding you are getting through your study of marriage only if you act as their teacher. Instead of just sitting back passively and letting in-laws take you or leave you, you must do something to foster their acceptance of you as a person, and to help them develop their positions and new roles created by your marriage. There is a very handy and useful technique for doing this if you can learn how to use it. It is called the "attitude technique."

Playing a role associated with a position in society is very little more than assuming the attitude that society expects a person in the given position to have. Everyone does a great deal of this kind of play-acting every day. The attitude of a high-school student toward his teachers is supposed to be one of respect. If you are smart, you assume this attitude no matter how you may feel inwardly about a given teacher. If you are a football player, you assume an attitude of extreme aggressiveness toward the member of the team opposite you, even though he may be your own brother and you have no feeling of anger or dislike for him whatsoever. You also use attitudes to convey ideas about your feelings and general personality even when they are not always exactly accurate in fact.

The useful thing about attitudes is that they tend to become real. The more you practice a positive, friendly attitude toward some individual, the more likely you and he are to become friends in truth. On the other hand, if you persistently appear to be disagreeable and suspicious of another person, he will get the idea that the dislike is real. He will assume the same attitude, and the first thing you know you have an enemy.

The same theory applies to in-laws if you really would like to be accepted by your father-in-law and mother-in-law and the rest of the kinfolk involved, and they really would like to feel that you accepted them. Nine times out of ten, though, the first positive move will be yours rather than theirs. After all, in a way, the son-in-law or daughter-in-law, or niece- or nephew-in-law, brother-in-law, sister-in-law, and so forth are the outsiders. Even under the most fortunate circumstances every new member of a family is on trial. If attitudes suggest acceptance and also convey the impression of being accepted, most of the problem is solved. Practice is important with attitudes, because people learn their societal roles and attitudes partly through experience in playing them.

You also learn how to play a societal role both from observation of others playing similar roles, and even more from observation of the way someone plays the complementary role involved. For example, you learn the role of daughter from having been a daughter, but that role is divided into the roles associated with being a daughter-of-a-mother and daughter-of-a-father. The same principle, of course, is true of the roles accompanying the position of son. If for one reason or another you have not had much experience with these positions, you will not know how to play them.

This is probably one of the reasons that researchers have found a high instance of "in-law trouble" when one or the other of the marriage team comes from a broken home. If you happen to fall into this category, however, you have a good defense against difficulty if you understand the use of positive attitudes in getting the experience necessary for playing a complementary in-law role.

Marriage often means that people in the extended family must learn to play new complementary roles. If a father-in-law has a family composed entirely of sons, he has had no experience with the roles associated with being father-of-a-daughter. He'll have to start from scratch in learning to be a father-in-law of a daughter-in-law. The mother-in-law is in exactly the same situation if she has had no experience in being a mother-of-a-daughter. Applying the same idea to all the other in-law relationships, you can speculate on what might be involved in various combinations. From your point of view, if you have never had a brother, brother-in-law roles in this family would be new to you. There are still other complications.

The new positions that come into existence as a result of marriage sometimes replace the old positions and sometimes are simply added to the old positions. As mentioned earlier, acceptance of new positions is part of the over-all acceptance in connection with in-laws. Normatively in our society, for instance, becoming a mother-of-a-married-son replaces being merely the mother-of-a-son. High up on the list of in-law problems, however, is the one created by the unwillingness or inability of some mothers to accept the new positions and roles in place of the old ones. For various psychological reasons it seems easier for fathers to accept their new position with respect to their sons or daughters than for mothers.

To make matters worse, some sons don't want their mothers to accept the new roles. This is not usual, but it is not uncommon either. You can easily see what the effect might be. Just imagine what happens when the son's mother continues to play the roles associated with motherhood to a son rather than those associated with being a mother to a married son, while at the same time the young wife wants to continue her old roles associated with being a daughter of her mother rather than a married daughter and wife. All this leads to a final practical observation about family relationships, both nuclear and extended.

The way you address people tends to suggest, and often to reflect, the way you feel about them—your attitude, in other words. Sociologists think the study of names for members of the extended family is important and have investigated it. They learned that many Americans *say* they call their parents-in-law "Mother" or "Father," sometimes modifying this by use of the last name—"Mother A" or "Father B." Observation, however, showed that although people *said* they used this form of address, large proportions of them did not actually use it. As a matter of fact, it appeared that a great many of those who were studied actually had no form of address at all for their parents-in-law, and simply grunted or mumbled when it was necessary to address them directly. These people, it was found, were more likely to have in-law problems than those who did actually use some fairly intimate name in addressing parents-in-law. These names might be anything from "Mother" and "Father" to "Mary" and "George," with assorted pet names in between. But researchers have also discovered that the names used for extended family members do not always indicate the emotional relationship in exactly the way one might expect.

An interesting illustration of this is the following quotation from a research report on use of names for kinsmen:

> . . . we ran across a number of situations of the following sort. An informant with three uncles would call one "John," one "Uncle Bill," and the other "Jim." When pressed to explain why he called the first uncle just plain "John," he would reply by saying that the person was a

LOVE AND MARRIAGE

> dirty so-and-so and that he would not dignify the man by calling him uncle. (This, by the way, was never said of mother or father.) The next question would be, "Well, how about your other uncle, Jim? Why don't you call him Uncle Jim?" And the explanation would be, "Jim is a wonderful guy! He and I have always been the closest friends. When I was a kid we would . . ." and out would come a picture of an idyllic relationship. The final question, of course, would be, "What about Uncle Bill?" And Uncle Bill would usually prove to be liked—a nice guy—"He's okay" or some such mildly positive or mildly negative sentiment.[11]

If the name does suggest an attitude, it may not, in the mind of the person using it, be the kind of attitude usually expected in connection with the name. But note that the researchers never found this mix-up in connection with a father or mother. There is no research to answer the question, but perhaps many people feel a kind of loyalty to their own parents, even when the relationship has been less than satisfactory, that makes it difficult to call somebody else "Father" or "Mother." This would account for the fact that so many who say they use these words actually do not. It would account, too, for the observed fact that many people, apparently almost with a sigh of relief, call their parents-in-law by the names their children use when they first begin to talk. This often results in some rather weird names.

The important point in connection with names for kinfolk is that they represent an area wherein the marriage team can and should make decisions early in marriage or even before. What you decide will be, in a subtle way, an expression of your attitude, and consequently it is likely to invoke a corresponding attitude. Here are two short anecdotes that show how things can work out. They also illustrate some other worthwhile points.

> Chuck is a jet pilot, flying an F-4C. (We tell you this simply because it gives a suggestion of the kind of man he is—and that's part of the idea in this illustration.)

FAMILY AND FAMILY ROLES

> *When he was a little boy, he called the husband of his mother's sister, "Uncle Zeke." He played catch a lot with Uncle Zeke.*
>
> *Uncle Zeke had been in the Air Corps during World War II. When Chuck started advanced pilot training, he began calling his uncle simply "Zeke" once in a while. When he got his wings, he dropped "uncle" entirely. After his tour in Vietnam, he got married to Ruth. Zeke and his wife couldn't be at the wedding; so Chuck and Ruth arranged their wedding trip to include a visit with them. The older couple had never met Ruth. Chuck introduced his new wife, who very politely shook hands with Uncle Zeke and Aunt Rose. They stayed four days. When they left, Ruth kissed Zeke and Rose. Uncle and Aunt had disappeared. Zeke and Rose think Ruth is wonderful.*

The other thumbnail sketch has to do with Dave and Nancy. Some things about it are unusual, but the sketch, like the one above, illustrates something more than just the choice and use of names.

> *The first time Dave asked Nancy for a date she had already agreed to go to a show with her parents. The usual thing, under the circumstances, would be to break the date with her parents or, if she wasn't very keen on dating Dave, to use them as an excuse for not going out with him. But for some reason she told Dave she'd date him if he'd go along with her and her parents to the show first. (Maybe she already had designs on him.) Dave thought this was about the craziest idea he'd ever heard of, but he went along with it. All four of them had a good time, and Dave had some time alone with Nancy afterward. A few months later, Nancy and Dave told her parents they were going to get married— they were engaged.*
>
> *After this news had been digested, Dave said something like this: "Now, another thing. I'd like permission to*

107

stop calling you 'Mr. and Mrs.' and instead use your first names. 'Father' and 'Mother' are too formal for friends!"

This sketch is given only as an illustration of what has been suggested throughout this discussion of the extended family. It may be summed up with the idea that, in the United States, the extended family is more a matter of friendship than of kinship.

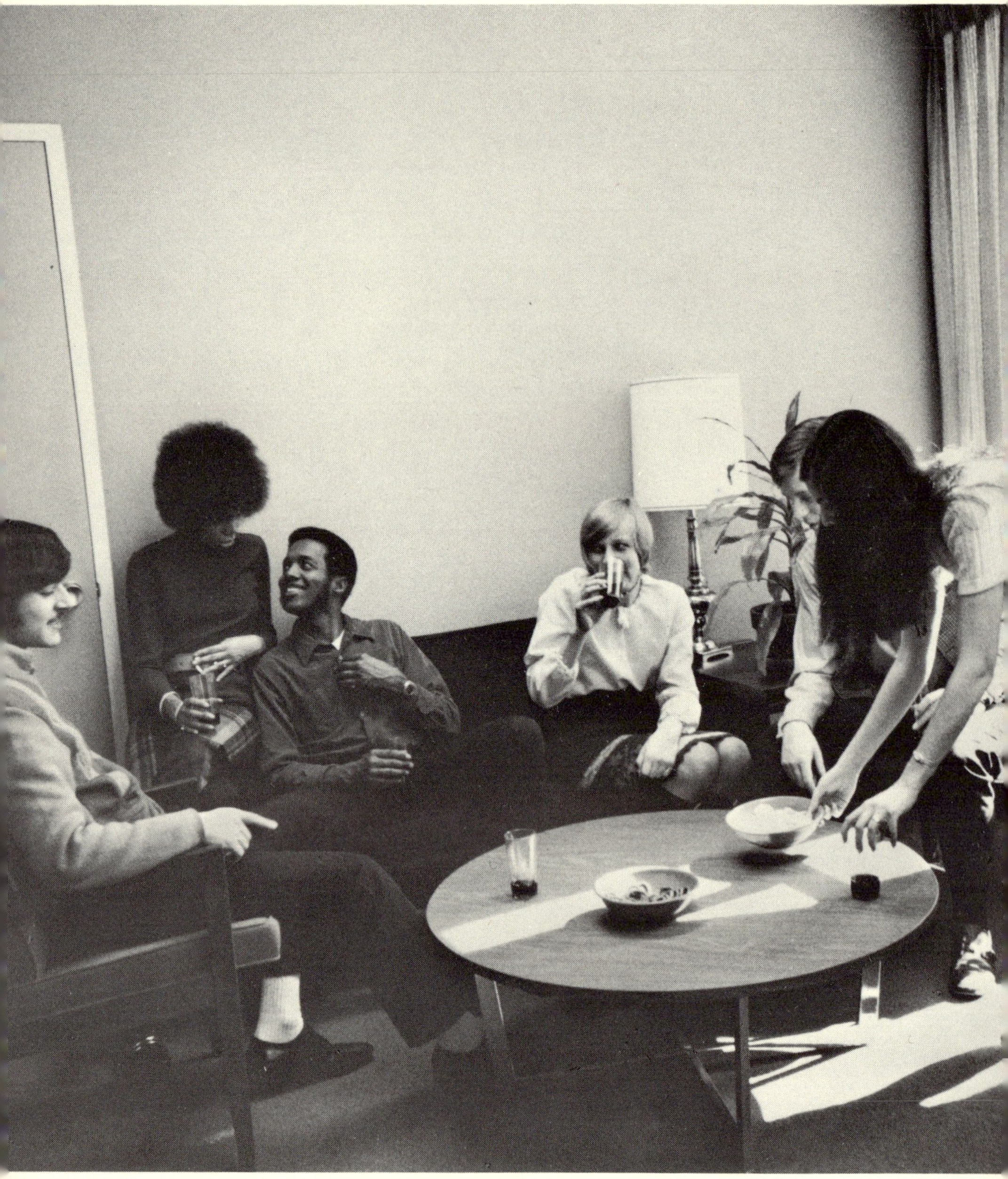

9

Neighbors and Friends

Your friend is your needs answered.

He is your field which you sow with love and reap with thanksgiving.

And he is your board and your fireside.

For you come to him with your hunger, and you seek him for peace.

When your friend speaks his mind you fear not the "nay" in your own mind, nor do you withhold the "ay."

And when he is silent your heart ceases not to listen to his heart;

For without words, in friendship, all thought, all desires, all expectations are born and shared, with joy that is unacclaimed.

. . .

And in the sweetness of friendship let there be laughter, and sharing of pleasures.
—KAHLIL GIBRAN: *The Prophet*

Human beings are social animals. They rely on other human beings to supply a great many of their needs, and emotionally they simply cannot endure isolation from other people very long. Every man and woman, therefore, interacts daily with other human beings, quite apart from members of the nuclear family. In this interaction they play what social scientists call *external roles*. These include the roles played in interaction with other people all the way from groceryman to in-laws, parents, and other kinfolk.

Although there might be interaction with certain people regardless of marriage, being married calls for normative roles different from those that are played in interaction with the same persons by unmarried men and women. It's obvious that interaction between two bachelors is likely to be different from interaction between two married men. And interaction between a married man and an unmarried woman (or vice versa) can present some difficulties, which may or may not be complicated according to the traditional romantic lines. Sex is not necessarily the crucial factor here. The difference in interaction may simply result from different feelings of responsibility and attitudes—ways of thinking. In addition, marriage creates a special list of roles that husband and wife play jointly in interaction with other couples and individuals outside the nuclear family or their own marriage relationship. Even when one marriage team interacts with another, each member of both teams must interact individually with each member of the other team. How he or she plays these interaction roles may profoundly affect interaction with the spouse, and it certainly affects the general atmosphere and flavor of marriage. In strangely subtle ways, the manner of playing all external roles affects marriage.

All external roles are played most smoothly in a *spirit* of friendship, but true friendship is not always necessary. Sometimes when it is involved, for the individual husband or wife, it may be more a liability than an asset. This is a significant matter for the marriage team to analyze, discuss, and make decisions about with respect to other people—couples or individuals—related to the external roles that must be played.

One key to the decision-making in this area is learning how to differentiate between neighbors and friends.

By standard definition, neighbors are families, couples, or individuals who live together in a more or less limited geographical area within a larger geographical area. This limited area is called a neighborhood, and the roles the people living there play in interaction with the other residents of the area are sometimes called neighboring roles.

Society as a whole is not entirely explicit and consistent about how neighboring roles should be played. Each separate neighborhood frequently has its own set of rules. When people have learned one set of rules in a particular neighborhood and then move to another with a different set of rules, there is conflict and perhaps unhappiness. The line from Robert Frost's poem "Mending Wall," "Good fences make good neighbors," expresses the idea that, even though living in close proximity, people get along better if they "keep to themselves." This philosophy is good as far as invasion of privacy, trespassing, and "butting in" are concerned.

On the other hand, self-imposed isolation is a way of life for many people, who may live next door in a residential district or apartment house for years and never even speak to their neighbors. A modern married couple used to this way of regarding neighbors may actually incur the enmity of people in their neighborhood by appearing to be snobbish or disdainful. If, however, a couple are used to the free and relatively unrestrained interchange of casual visits, they too may be rejected where the code is "Good fences make good neighbors," because they appear to be pushing and ill-mannered. Each neighborhood has its own set of rules for neighboring, and recognition of the code is essential.

In general, however, modern neighboring is a sort of compromise between these two extremes, plus a measure of selectivity regarding those with whom neighboring is shared.

Modern selective neighboring is different from traditional neighboring in several ways, but the basic principles are the same. Neighbors help each other, borrow and lend food and materials, and try to maintain comparable standards of housekeeping and dwelling-place upkeep. Their children play together, and each set of parents feels some responsibility for the neighbors' children. Wives and husbands, individually and together, visit back and forth. Nevertheless, modern transportation and communication devices like automobiles and telephones have gone a long way toward breaking down the idea of neighbors being only people who live in a restricted geographical area. In addition, many of the needs of people are met by social organizations that serve a much larger area than the traditional one. Interactions and external roles are spread more widely than they once were; they include more people more widely separated.

Today we tend to think of members of the larger community, such as a city, a town, a state, or even a region, as neighbors. In addition, neighbors and neighboring may involve external roles dictated by close association in a job or occupation, a fraternal organization, a church, a school or college, or any other kind of situation that brings families, couples, or individuals together frequently and regularly.

Neighbors, then, are people who, because of some degree of geographical proximity share certain common interests. These interests usually center on a feeling of pride or understanding about the area, large or small, in which they live; a sense of responsibility for cooperating with others in the same area for mutual advantage; frequently, but not inevitably, some exchange of amenities; and a general feeling of trust and confidence in the other people who live in the neighborhood. In a neighborhood where all or some of these attributes are not present, there is likely to be little neighboring. This makes choice of neighborhood an important matter for decision by a young marriage team.

On one hand, their social growth and development could be nipped in the bud by a careless decision. They could become isolated, with few opportunities for playing some of the external roles necessary for emotionally healthy life. On the other hand, there can be some real problems when there is no clearly drawn line between neighboring and friendship.

Friendship frequently begins with some kind of neighboring. Whether you think about pre-marriage friends or post-marriage friends, couple friends or separate individual friends, they must develop from a situation that involves interaction, initially based on frequent and more or less regular contact. But neighboring does not necessarily produce friendships, and friendship, after it is established, does not necessarily involve continued neighboring—as when friends live in different towns, for instance. There are several characteristics of friendship that distinguish it from the relationships that may be formed in the course of neighboring. First, friends share common interests. This does not mean that all their interests are exactly the same. It simply means that there is at least enough commonality to make conversation and exchange of ideas mutually interesting and challenging. Either agreement or disagreement on politics, religion, economics, or a host of other matters may be the basis for initial friendship. Interest in the subject and the ability to communicate are the essentials.

In the first stage, the relative importance and significance of the common interests make all the difference between neighbors and friends. The shared interests may spring only from the fact that people live in the same geographical area and are concerned, in the interrelationship, only with "neighborhood problems." Neighbors may be interested in matters that do not extend beyond the fact that they happen to be more or less forced to see each other and communicate about something. This is not really a friendship stage—even at the first level.

Friends also share pleasures over and above their common interests. These pleasures may be simply old-fashioned visiting, if it is lively, or playing cards or golf, fishing, hunting, shopping, or almost anything that is done *together*. Sharing a good meal is the most ancient and time-honored token of friendship.

The third characteristic of friendship is a little less simple. Friends count on each other for help in practically every possible way. Most importantly, people not only expect the help of their friends, they also count on their friends asking them for help. Friendship involves as much giving as it does receiving. Many friendships have been nipped in the bud because one of the parties involved did not ask the other for help when he needed it. Of course, the kind of help asked for is critical. Friends don't ask each other for unreasonable help, or for something that might create hardship for the person who is asked to help. Friends never really impose, but at the same time they assume that a request is not always an imposition.

Friends understand and accept each other's strengths and weaknesses and differences in points of view, beliefs, or feelings. Of course, they may argue and disagree, but with friends this is not a damaging factor. Friends recognize and respect their differences and accept each other as they are—the bad along with the good.

Friends trust each other. They don't let each other down. If one says he will do something for the other, both know he will do what he says. Along with this goes trust that confidences and secrets can be safely shared. Friends don't betray each other. Each knows, somehow, that the other has his welfare as much at heart as his own.

The sixth and most significant characteristic of true friendship is the ability to understand and share thoughts, ideas, and ideals through a special process of communication that really can not be described in simple words. Psychologists call this rare ability *empathy*. It means that a person understands the feelings and shares the experiences of another person without exactly knowing how he does it. It is a kind of communication without words. This relationship applies chiefly to individual, person-to-person relationships, but it can also apply to the relationship of the marriage team with friends and neighbors of both members.

The use of a friendship scale can be very helpful in making some marriage decisions, because one important decision may be the relationships between the team and the friends and neighbors. There will, inevitably, be neighbors, but whether or not they will also be friends is something that must be discussed and decided.

Roughly, the friendship scale corresponds to the six characteristics of friendship. It is a six-step scale in which each step, except of course the first, adds a new characteristic to all the preceding ones. The characteristics are, briefly:

1. Common interests
2. The sharing of pleasures
3. Mutual help and support
4. Acceptance of faults and disagreements
5. Trust
6. Empathy

The first grade of friendship, then, is simply number one above: the sharing of common interests. Then the scale goes on like this:

Grade 2 = 1 + 2
Grade 3 = 1 + 2 + 3
Grade 4 = 1 + 2 + 3 + 4
Grade 5 = 1 + 2 + 3 + 4 + 5
Grade 6 = 1 + 2 + 3 + 4 + 5 + 6

When all these characteristics are present, the result is true friendship. There are almost infinite degrees of intensity or quality in each of them. You can't measure these degrees; you can only feel them. In the development of friendship, you can't safely assume there is an orderly progression from one grade to the next. The grades of friendship can get mixed up, so that some of the more advanced characteristics sometimes seem to be present before the earlier ones have developed.

Whose friends are they? Are they yours, mine, or ours? The answer, in a nutshell, is that *they* are *our* friends. But there is a difference between this answer and those in relation to income, leisure time, and family. The difference is that the friendship grade almost certainly will not be the same for both you and your marriage partner.

Every individual is entitled to his own personal friends of any of the six grades. The common interests that either marriage partner shares with a friend or friends may well not be shared with the other partner. Husbands may have hunting and fishing friends, poker-playing friends, or hobby friends in scores of categories. Wives share common interests and meet the other higher-grade requirements of friendship with other women. This is normal and healthy. Each member of the marriage team must accept these facts. But when an individual friendship of one member of the team appears to be threatening in any way to the other member, it's time to put the team process into operation. The dangers lie chiefly, perhaps, in the stages where shared pleasures, confidences, and secrets are involved.

If the team cannot agree that the friends are *ours*, even though the friendship grades are different, the individual friend relationship can be very damaging to the marriage, and perhaps should be given up as quickly and smoothly as possible. This principle applies to both pre-marriage and post-marriage individual friends of either marriage partner. It applies also to friendships with other couples.

One problem in couple friendships comes from the difficulty in distinguishing accurately between true common interests—those shared by everyone involved—and mere habitual common activity. Couples who play cards together, invite each other to meals more or less regularly, or do many other possible things together are not necessarily friends. Sharing activities is not the same thing as having common interests. It may be the starting point for true couple friendship, but in itself it is only a starting point.

If shared activities of couples are no more than superficial suggestions of common interests, they can be detrimental to marriage. In the first place, if they become habitual, which they tend to do, they can upset the leisure time and the dollar budgets. The returns, in terms of friendship, are not worth the costs, in dollars and use of leisure. This is particularly true in the period of establishment, but it works out in other ways in later stages of marriage.

If superficial shared activities are mistaken for friendship and true couple friendship is not established, the relationship between couples is especially vulnerable to the possibility that as time goes on one couple will have a much larger dollar income than the other. This leads to the age-old process of "keeping up with the Joneses," which fosters more marital trouble than you might believe possible. If true couple friendship exists, the increasing dollar income of one couple over another will make little or no difference. The more affluent couple may even be a resource for the less affluent couple in many ways other than actually giving or lending money, which usually ends all semblance of friendship abruptly. But if the couple relationship involves rivalry, it is not really a friendship. During the period of establishment, the selection of couple friends and distinguishing between friends and sharers of activities is very important.

You and your partner can select your friends just about as objectively, using the team process, as you might select a new automobile. As a matter of fact, some of the considerations, such as durability and cost of upkeep, are the same for friends and automobiles. There is one difference—you can't select friends unless they select you, too.

To begin with, think of people that you and your marriage partner believe are worth spending a little time with. Then you apply in a deliberate and objective way some of the basic principles just discussed. Through discussion, the marriage team answers several vital questions:

1. Do we think of the other couple as potential friends simply because they happen to be handy or seem to like us?

2. Can we afford to pursue this potential friendship? You know that it is going to cost something for entertainment, both in money and in time. You have to decide, on the basis of what you can observe, whether or not you'll be able to keep up your end. If it matters to you that the other couple drives a brand-new Ford Mustang while you have a six-year-old Volkswagen—or if this matters to the potential friends—you'd probably better call the whole thing off before it goes any farther. If these things don't really matter to either of you or to the other couple, it may work out that this in itself is a good basis for friendship. But remember the basic principles of friendship as contrasted with neighboring.

3. What are the chances of the potential friendship being relatively permanent? In modern living this is not only an im-

portant question but is also a very difficult one to answer. True friendship, whether it involves individual members of the marriage team or both members, must be lasting. In selecting friends and committing yourself and your marriage partner to the requirements and the expectations of friendship, it is a good idea to consider whether or not the friendship is likely to be a matter of here today and gone tomorrow.

4. This question is sometimes the most perplexing, complicated, and important of all. It has to do with decisions about pre-marriage friends of any grade above number-one. It is a question that cannot even be asked clearly and succinctly, because there are so many possibilities. Suppose, for instance, that either member of the marriage team had a grade-five or grade-six friendship before marriage with someone of the same sex, and that the other marriage partner doesn't like that friend at all. Couple friendship is obviously impossible; but does the partner directly involved pretend, adjust, or end the original friendship abruptly and definitely?

Another possibility is that both members of the marriage team were pre-marriage friends of both members of another team. All is well until, perhaps, the common interests on which the first friendships were based change. One couple has children; the other doesn't, or not until much later. One husband goes into selling insurance; the other joins the Navy. One wife works; the other plays bridge for recreation. When things like these happen, the pre-marriage friendships are likely to fade away, usually painlessly, unless there is a stubborn and mistaken loyalty simply because the friendship once existed.

There is still another kind of situation. Suppose the pre-marriage friendship at a top-level stage involved, for either member of the team, a person of the opposite sex. Suppose, too, this pre-marriage friend marries and becomes a sufficiently close neighbor to establish a possible couple friendship. There are no pat answers to any of the questions suggested by these situations. Everything depends on the honest, smooth-working, marriage team process.

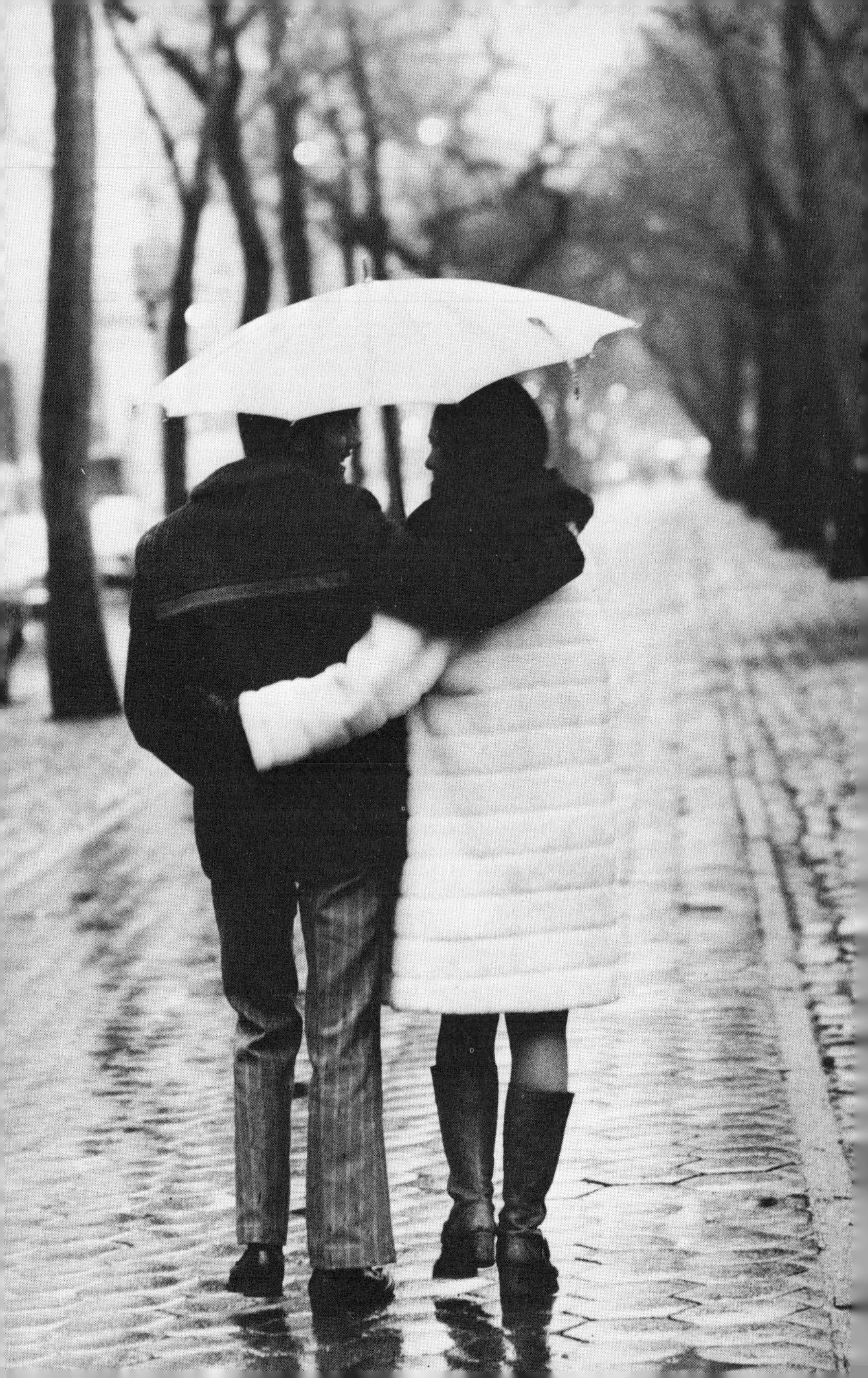

10

Love

> If you have to acknowledge that you have been neglectful of the frail but fragrant flower of love, I would ask you to remember that your time is, after all, your life. As the moments tick by, and the sand runs swiftly through the hour-glass, it is life itself that is slowly slipping away. You take time to work and time to play, time to eat and time to sleep, time for personal interests and time for social responsibilities. Surely, in all this wealth of time which is you, you can take time to keep in love.
> —DAVID R. MACE: *Success in Marriage*

It is probably safe to say that more has been written about love, with less agreement, than about any other subject with which men and women have busied their pens and typewriters. Although everyone has had experience with an emotion he thought of as love, such wide disagreement in thinking about love is understandable because there are many different reasons for writing about love. Some philosophers and poets are interested in love as an abstract force influencing mankind everywhere. Social scientists may be interested in love of friends, regardless of sex, or in the part that love plays in parent-child relationships. Still others are interested in love as a basis for mate selection, or pre-marital or extra-marital sex. This chapter is concerned with the love of husband and wife.

The following definitions of love are particularly appropriate to married love, although they may be applied to love in general.

> *Love is the relationship between one person and another which is most conducive to the optimal [best possible] development of both.*[12]
>
> *. . . love is an activity, not a passion . . . the essence of love is to labor for something, to make something grow. . . . Love is the expression of intimacy between two human beings under the condition of the preservation of each other's integrity . . .*[13]
>
> *. . . love is defined as a strong emotional attachment . . . between adolescents or adults of opposite sexes, with at least the components of sex desire and tenderness.*[14]

These three definitions include what most social scientists and philosophers would accept as the basic components of married love at its best. True, there are many other definitions that diverge from these three—many of them cynical—but these definitions cover the most significant points agreed upon by most people who have studied love.

1. Love, like friendship, is unselfish. In love, as in friendship, each party gets as much as the other. Friendship and love both involve sacrifice, but the sacrifice gives pleasure and helps the growth and development of the one who makes it as much as that of the one for whom the sacrifice is made.
2. Love is tender; it tries to avoid giving pain to the loved one.
3. Love is an emotion rather than a passion.
4. Married love involves sex and sex desire.
5. Love is a process of development; it either grows or it dies.

Married love is a continuing process of learning how to apply these basic principles most effectively throughout the marriage cycle. These characteristics are usually not all present at the same time and with the same intensity or quality—especially in the period of establishment. The whole secret of successful married love is to work constantly toward applying them steadily from the day of marriage to the day of death.

Underlying all the definitions of love and the five principles they involve is the same requirement that was listed for grade-six friendship—empathy. One writer has this to say about empathy:

> *If another person matters as much to you as you do yourself, it is quite possible to talk to this person as you have never talked to anyone before. The freedom which comes . . . permits [shades] of meaning, permits investigation without fear of rebuff which greatly augments [discussion and agreement about] all sorts of things.*[15]

Empathy is not something you get all of a sudden. True, you may meet a person and say to yourself unconsciously, "This is someone with whom I might achieve empathy." Leaving out the matter of sexual attraction, this is what is meant by "falling in love." Actually, you don't fall in love at first sight, romantic notions to the contrary. Neither do you "fall in empathy" at first sight. Empathy has to be achieved—learned, developed, deliberately cultivated. It comes from practice and experience. And even though empathy has been described as silent communication, learning how to achieve it involves communication through words and actions.

Love is not a simple declaration of passion or desire by one party. It involves both giving and receiving, and in giving the lover also receives. You can't actually love somebody who hardly knows you exist, although the feeling of love can be extended to include all mankind. As one writer has suggested, however, this is a sort of "saintly love," which illustrates without really defining love as it is experienced by most people. The concern here, however, is love of one person for another, and this is impossible unless it is reciprocated. It involves being together, just as friendship does. Without this togetherness and interaction, what sometimes passes for love is only a kind of fantasy. This does not mean that love requires the continued and constant physical presence of lover and loved one. Love withstands separation, if communication and interaction continue. Without interaction and communication, separation, as in death, offers only the possibility of remembered love.

There is another point to be made about reciprocity of love. If another person matters as much to you as you do to yourself, the value of the relationship depends as much on the importance you attach to yourself as it does on the importance of the other person.

Americans assert, theoretically at least, that marriage is based on love, but some cultures have made little or no pretense about marriage for love. Marriages are arranged on economic or other bases. This does not preclude love, in some stage or degree before or after marriage; but a look at the potentials can help greatly in understanding aspects of modern love in marriage. A contemporary musical play, *Fiddler on the Roof*, gives some insight that should be useful. The setting of this play is a Russian village peopled almost entirely by Jews. The time is the very early twentieth century when Russia was still ruled by the Czar.

Orthodox Jewish culture offers a rather good example of our marriage team idea, with some superficial differences. The father is supposed to be the supreme authority in the family, but in practice it is understood that the husband and wife share the power. The Jews developed a close approximation of equalitarian marriage long before some of the other cultures, although it did not include freedom of choice in mate selection until modern times.

The culture of the village in *Fiddler on the Roof* dictates that marriages are to be arranged by a professional matchmaker acting as go-between for the parents of the two individuals for whom marriage was proposed. Traditionally, of course, matchmaking involved a good deal of bargaining and dickering. It had always been a tradition, and love had never been included among the considerations. But in the play we see the beginnings of a change. Central characters in the play are a milkman, who delivers his milk in an old rickety horse-drawn cart, and his wife, Goldie. They have three daughters, all of marriageable age. One of the daughters, Hilda, violates tradition by falling in love with a poor young man and the two of them bravely approach the father to ask permission to become engaged. The father is astounded, shocked, and at first angry. But as he thinks of his daughter and her happiness and listens to their explanations of how they feel about each other, he begins to believe they may have some valid arguments on their side and decides to violate tradition by allowing the engagement without going through the official village matchmaker.

Marriage teamwork is in itself one expression of love, because it involves such elements of love as the sharing of common interests, trust, and empathy. The marriage team is not only a decision-making, policy-setting team, but also a team for keeping love alive and growing. This requires something a little different from other team operations. There are different roles to play.

Since love involves both giving and receiving, each member of the marriage team has two possible sets of roles to be played in expressing love—the role of giver and the role of receiver. Of course, by definition, love as an emotion is shared by both husband and wife. There are, or should be, situations or circumstances in married life when the giving and receiving are simultaneous, when giving and receiving for both husband and wife are blended together. But in overt acts that carry the message, "I love you," one person plays the role of giver, and to make communication complete the other must play the role of receiver. The latter is the more difficult.

The role of receiver of expressions of love involves communicating to the giver a sense of understanding that the expression of love is not taken for granted or as a kind of reward. An expression of love received as if it were only something rightfully and justly due is not likely to contribute much to the continuation and growth of love. The role of receiver is a difficult one for which there are no standard rules or patterns. Each marriage team has to work out its own code for communicating in such a way that the receiver turns the receipt itself into an expression of love.

The general principle underlying expression of love in marriage is continuation of the courtship. In a literal sense, of course, this is extremely unrealistic, and the more romantic the courtship, the more unrealistic the idea. Some disillusionment is inevitable after the rosy glow of the first part of the period of establishment. By recognizing some of the causes of disillusionment, you can better understand how married courtship can be possible.

In the period during which love developed, practically all the time you and your marriage partner spent together was leisure time, and you probably spent much of it outside the home. After marriage you and your partner spend more time together than before, but less is leisure time and still less is outside the home.

In courtship, then, most of the time you spent together required mutual recognition of each other's presence. Practically everything you did together involved the other person closely. In marriage, both of you are almost forced to be more preoccupied with your own affairs when you are with your partner than you were in courtship. This is more likely, perhaps, to be true of husbands than of wives, but the principle applies to both. What can the team do about it? There have been a number of studies of married life and love that suggest answers.

One study investigates the way in which husbands report to wives about their activities during the working day. The study found that in the first three years of marriage husbands usually talk with their wives about activities outside the home at least once a day. Then after the arrival of the first child or approximately after the first three years of marriage, they do this only a few times a week. At later stages the reports dwindle off to less than one a week and from then on the frequency declines virtually to zero.

Another study focused on wives rather than husbands. It asked how frequently wives tell their husbands about the problems they encountered during the day or their problems in general. The study found that only 22 percent of the wives always talked over their troubles with their husbands, and that 9 percent of them never did.

Both of these studies illustrate ways in which love may be expressed by mutual recognition. Each partner plays both roles—giver and receiver. The team's function is to establish positive ways of reversing the trends shown in these investigations.

Still another study found out how happily married couples mutually rated their pleasures in certain leisure time activities. The results showed this pattern:

> Listening to the radio* 90%
> Music 89%
> Reading 72%
> Movies 68%

> * The study was made before TV largely replaced radio. The figure might apply to TV.

Other leisure time activities were social and not applicable here; but the reported enjoyment of both partners steadily declined. The items noted here head the list of all the activities and suggest how important the *sharing* of leisure time pleasures may be, especially if real empathy has been achieved. Note, too, that with the possible exception of reading, these activities are often associated with courtship. The idea of courtship in marriage works in other ways, too.

Celebrating the past by remembering the anniversaries and milestones in the development of the original love is one form of expressing love or of keeping it alive. It is perhaps more significant for wives than it is for husbands. One writer on marriage has observed the importance of celebrating the past in this passage:

> . . . To be sure, the fever-pitch of pre-marital romance can never be fully revived. But the memory of the golden age when love was new is worth preserving and recalling. This is the function of wedding anniversaries, not simply to celebrate a date on the calendar but to recreate old times, revisit the scenes of courtship, replay the old love songs. If marriage is worth celebrating with a reception and a honeymoon, it is also worth re-celebrating from year to year.
>
> The past is worth recapturing not only in terms of the

> climactic wedding event but also in the whole pattern of dating. Repeating treasured experiences of courtship is likely to recall old feelings of love. Going dancing again or to a dinner or a show has extra value if it repeats an activity that was relished in the past.
>
> Romantic occasions not only recreate the past but also create in the present. Love is enhanced by the little extras we label "romantic"—the candles on the table, the flowers, the gifts, the dressing up. These may be mere symbols of love, but they express it more visibly than words and help create a mood of appreciation.[16]

Recalling the past is often a private matter between husband and wife, but when it is shared as much as possible with children, it also helps to give children an idea of the importance of marriage and love that will help them in their own adult lives.

Children loom very large on the screen of love expression. Sometimes they are referred to as "tokens of love" in themselves, although this implies a value assigned to children rather than to marriage itself or love between the marriage partners. There is no escaping the fact, however, that children are a possible force for or obstacle to a continuing and growing love, requiring a marriage team to understand the situation and work intelligently to deal with it. This certainly does not mean that the marriage team has to make a decision between continuing love and having children. Quite the reverse! Children offer both a test of the love of husband and wife and a means of strengthening it. At the same time, children do make it necessary to readjust the ways in which love between husband and wife is expressed.

In the first place, children inevitably interfere with the privacy between husband and wife. Many expressions of love, aside from the sexual, including the post-marriage dating activities, call for a certain degree of privacy, or for the two members of the marriage team to be alone together even if they are alone together in a crowd. A good deal of love expression may depend on, or be considerably aided by, the house or apartment in which the married couple lives. It may also depend upon the availability of babysitters, which gives the couple an occasional chance to be by themselves. The point simply is that if childen completely dominate the domestic scene, the continued expressions of love which keep it alive and growing may be difficult or impossible.

Young children require a great deal of mothering even after they are old enough to go to school. This is true even when the mother is employed in a job outside the home, either part-time or full-time. The question is, if love between husband and wife depends upon sharing of interests and activities as well as the opportunity for personal and private communication, what is the father going to do to hold up his end of the requirements when the children are young?

Of course, if he does his best in his job, and the mother does her best in her job, each has a sense of contribution, which is in itself an expression of love. But probably the most important contribution the father can make is to demonstrate his understanding of the demands of mothering and his appreciation of the quality of the mother's performance. Another expression of love which a husband can make is to help all he can in the child-rearing process, even though this is possible only in his off-work hours.

There is another way in which children affect the expression of love and even the love of husband and wife itself. This is the transfer of one love to another—the love of husband for wife or wife for husband to the love of children. A kind of rivalry sometimes develops at the expense of husband-wife love. One task of the marriage team, working as a team, is to see that their own love relationship is strengthened rather than weakened by the presence of children.

Physical expressions of love are very important in the development of love in marriage. A good-morning kiss or a good-night kiss, with some others thrown in between, are very important ways of expressing love. Holding hands or administering an affectionate pat or looking fondly at each other come under this category also. These physical expressions of love go a long way toward teaching the children, very subtly, some elements of marriage and love relationships that they need to learn.

Sexual intercourse can be an expression of love in marriage. In fact, it is frequently called the most complete or "finest" way of communicating love between a man and a woman. It is not always an expression of love, even in marriage, and when it is, the expression may sometimes be a very complicated sort of communication. There are more overtones and varieties of meaning of love involved in this means of expression than in any of the others.

Sexual intercourse as as expression of love is possible only if all or most of the other expressions are also used. In other words, sexual intercourse alone won't keep love alive. But it is a fundamental factor in marriage.

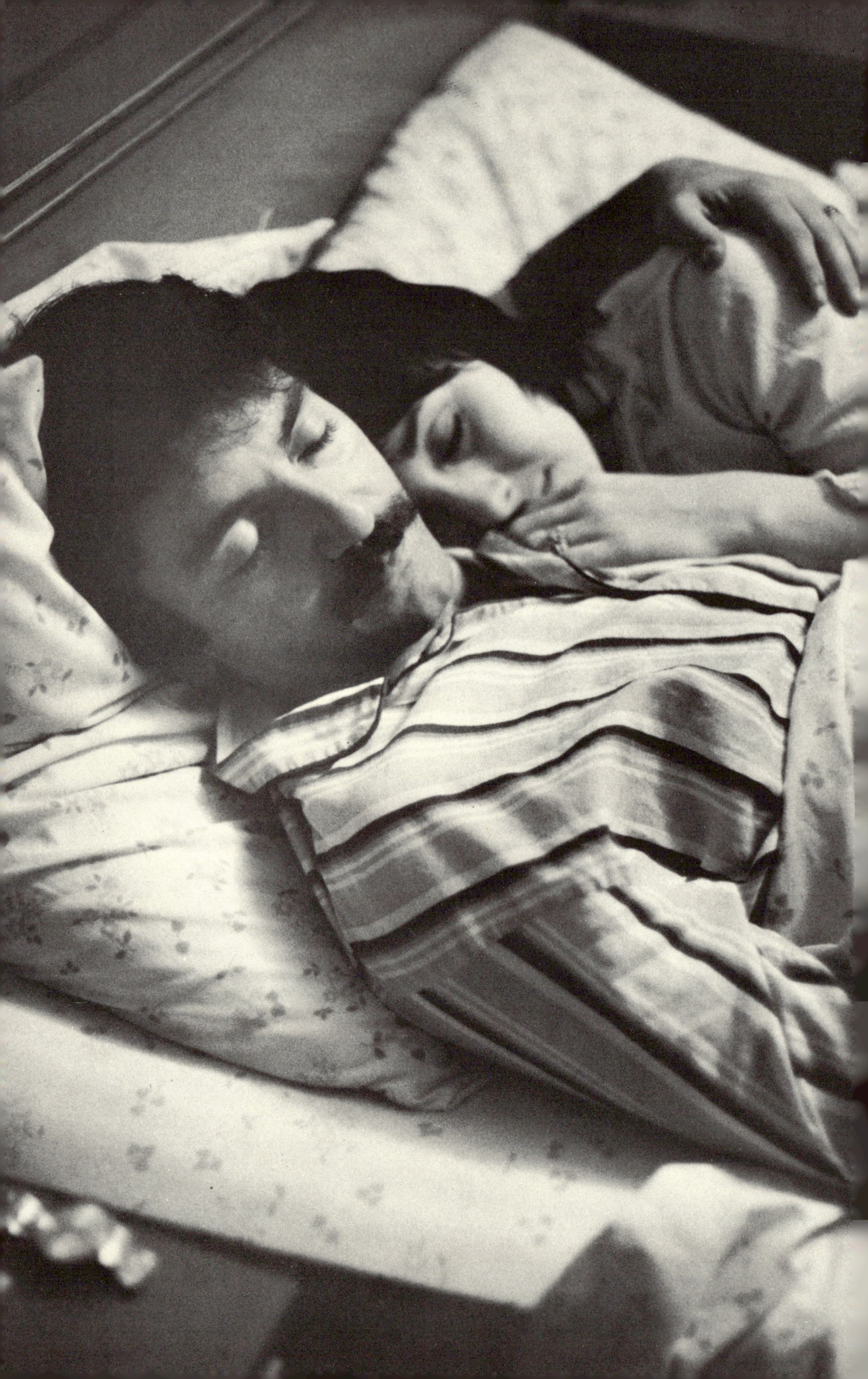

11

Sex and Marriage

> Here, where I trace your body with my hand,
> Love's presence has no end;
> For these, your arms that hold me, are the world's.
> In us, the continents, clouds and oceans meet
> Our arbitrary selves, extensive with the night,
> Lost, in the heart's worship, and the body's sleep.
> —KATHLEEN RAINE: "Love Poem"

Sex and the sex act combine to form the most versatile form of communication known to man. The messages transmitted by sex are so subtle they usually cannot be translated into words in any language. They may range all the way from an expression of hate to the most eloquent expression of love. In between, sex may express disdain, selfishness or unselfishness, unconcern, apathy—virtually every emotion, feeling, and need of a human being.

Sex may also express tenderness, compassion, reverence, companionship, and just about all the emotions and feelings that make life worth living. Sex, in many ways, is the central focus of human existence.

Sexual intercourse in marriage may possibly express all the negative feelings and emotions listed above, but only in marriage is it so likely to express the positive aspects of sexual intercourse. However, for many married couples there is a possibility that their sex in marriage becomes so casual and routine and disregardful of the other partner that its value is simply lost in a virtual haze of habit. A thought-provoking comment in this connection was made by a unmarried college girl who is quoted as having said:

> One thing, though. I really miss necking. Sex is so casual and taken for granted—I mean we go to dinner, we go home, get undressed like old married people, you know—and just go to bed. It's really like a marriage-type thing. I mean I'm not saying I'd like to be raped on the living room floor exactly. But I would love to just sit around on the sofa and neck.[17]

This statement does not by any means accurately describe sex in marriage. It does, however, indicate what sexual intercourse sometimes is like for all married people, and what it is like for some married people all or most of the time. It also suggests, without meaning to, a good deal about how sexual interaction in marriage can be developed into something a lot more satisfying than it sometimes is. What the researchers call "sexual adjustment" is still one of the major factors in successful marriage.

Despite the sexual revolution supposedly under way, sex in marriage involves for countless men and women aspects of fear, feelings of inadequacy and separateness, which are harmful to the marriage relationship and the marriage team. Perhaps this comes from confusing the word *sex*—something one does—with something that one is.

Sexual adjustment in marriage is a matter of sexual interaction, which includes, but is not limited to, sexual intercourse itself. Sexual interaction is the total pattern of sexual expression of both husband and wife, along with a mutual understanding of sexual needs. Sexual interaction involves both the expression of sexual needs and the response to the expression. The fact that this interaction is present more or less all of the time in marriage—sometimes in the background and sometimes in the very forefront of husband-wife relationships, makes sex in marriage different from sex outside marriage. Sexual intercourse, resulting from sexual interaction, is always an immediate possibility. Outside of marriage it is also a possibility, but not an ever-present one, and it is seldom an integral part of the lives of two people outside of marriage, as it is in marriage. Furthermore, sexual intercourse in marriage has many more uses than it has outside of marriage.

Especially in marriage, sex involves not only the techniques of sexual intercourse, but also the understanding of male and female differences psychologically and socially. The statement of the unmarried college girl quoted above subtly illustrates the point. She wants what she thinks of as romanticism in her affair, and she believes that marriage destroys the romantic possibilities of her relationship with a boy who, presumably, is chiefly interested in the satisfaction of his sexual needs and desires.

The primary use of sexual intercourse is for the propagation of the species. This is called the biological purpose of sexual intercourse. It can be the sole, or the basic, use of sexual intercourse for a married couple at specific times. Theoretically, for some people it is the only justifiable purpose of sexual intercourse. This is the official position of the Roman Catholic church and of some other religions.

Even if sex is limited to a basic biological use, it is necessary to take into account very complicated factors about reasons for the limitations. In other words, the reasons for desiring children are important. There are probably very few men and women who deliberately set out to produce another human being just for the sake of adding to the already over-large population of the world. Husbands and wives in all cultures usually want children for many reasons, which will be discussed in a later chapter.

In the beginning of this chapter sexual intercourse was described as a means of expressing emotions. Its use as an expression of love is shown in the following passage:

> *Sexual intercourse may be said to be one aspect, perhaps the most basic and most important aspect, of a relationship between persons. In ideally mature form it is a relationship between a man and a woman in which*

> *giving and taking is equal, and in which the genitals are the most important channel through which love is expressed and received. It is one of the most natural, and certainly the most rewarding and the most life-enhancing of all human experiences. It is also the only one which both has a completely satisfying ending and yet can be endlessly repeated. Not even the greatest works of literature and music can stand such iteration. But this wonderfully enriching experience is only possible when the two people concerned have achieved a relationship in which, at least during the actual process of love-making, each is able to confront the other exactly as they are, with no reserves and no pretenses, and in which there is no admixture of childish dependence or fear.*[18]

Sexual intercourse does not always express love in this way. In marriage any single occasion of sexual intercourse may express some emotion or feeling different from those expressed in other occasions. Psychiatrists find situations in marriage when sexual intercourse is actually used as an expression of dislike or disdain.

Without going to this pathological extreme, sexual intercourse may, for example, be used as an expression of contrition after a husband-wife quarrel. Either the husband or the wife may use sexual intercourse to express irritation, anger, or forgiveness. It is important to understand that sexual intercourse is not always an expression of love, at least not in the way it is described in the quotation at the beginning of this chapter. It is also important to realize that sexual intercourse that does not match the description in the quotation is not less valuable, less satisfying or less good, because sexual intercourse has still other uses.

For both men and women, although perhaps more usually for men, sexual intercourse can be more effective than the most potent tranquilizer in reducing both nervous and physical tension. This use will be clearer when the neurology of sex is explained.

Sexual intercourse can be a wildly exciting experience, but at times a smooth-working marriage team may use it deliberately and satisfyingly in about the same spirit in which they might "take a couple of aspirins." This is one of the chief differences between sexual intercourse in marriage and sexual intercourse outside of marriage, and it does not detract in any way from the view of intercourse as a "noble" or "spiritual" experience. Strangely, this use of sexual intercourse is seldom openly recognized in books and articles about sex in marriage. It is, however, unquestionably recognized, consciously or unconsciously, by most happily married couples. Love can be expressed through sexual intercourse without mutual sexual passion.

Still another use of sexual intercourse is for pleasure. This use causes the most difficulty and can create the problem of sexual adjustment in marriage. Sex can be fun, but frankly it is not always fun for both partners. Even when it is, the pleasures of sexual intercourse are not necessarily the same for both male and female.

Two cultural forces are involved in this use of sexual intercourse. One of them is the underlying idea that sexual intercourse is not for pleasure alone, that it must be an expression of love or based on biological considerations. The other is that if pleasure is the purpose, there should be complete equality between the sexes in this pleasurable activity.

Our culture places particular emphasis on sex equality in voting, property ownership, and general status. It is only natural, then, that we should value the equal pleasure of sexual intercourse for both male and female. That is, sexual desires, pleasures, satisfactions, and the rights to achieve these should be equal for husband and wife.

Because this kind of equality has become almost a fetish, failure to achieve equal sexual satisfactions in marriage seems to indicate a fault of some sort in either the husband or the wife or in their so-called "techniques" in sexual intercourse. The basic value of equality and freedom is translated into the value of sexual equality, with respect to roles and rights, and from this into a value involving sexual equality where the pleasures of sexual intercourse are involved. For the middle class in America, this has become a prime factor in married sex. All class cultures expect at least some sharing of pleasure, even if not equality in sexual intercourse. This means you should know what is involved in the pleasures of sex; and what happens, neurologically, when pleasure or satisfaction results from sexual intercourse.

The neurological aspect of intercourse centers on orgasm, the focal point of all the uses of sexual intercourse from biological to pleasurable.

This introduces a complicated subject. The first thing to understand, very definitely, is that although orgasm in general is a focal point of all the uses of sex, it's the male orgasm that counts biologically. All the uses of sexual intercourse for both male and female are based on this. But the need for orgasm is much more insistent for males than for females. The feeling of need for orgasm develops much more slowly in females than for males, and is, in general, not so frequent. And as a matter of fact, sexual intercourse may be pleasant and rewarding to a woman even without orgasm.

Any of literally hundreds of possible stimuli can cause the male penis to become erect and firm. This makes it possible for the penis to penetrate the vagina of the female. Sometimes men experience erections involuntarily, even when actual sexual intercourse is not in prospect. Eventually, the tension and readiness for sexual intercourse throughout the entire nervous and vascular system of the male will subside. While it exists, the male is strongly impelled to relieve it. He can do this through sexual intercourse, through masturbation, or by simply ignoring it.

On the underside of the erect penis is an area called the glans penis which is extremely sensitive. Stimulation of this area by friction, either manually or in intercourse, brings about a release of the tension in a kind of explosion accompanied by a discharge of seminal fluid from the penis. This fluid contains millions of tiny cells called sperm. The expulsion of the seminal fluid is called ejaculation, and the total experience of tension relief and ejaculation is called orgasm. Orgasm is accompanied by an intense, indescribable feeling of pleasure and is followed by a relaxation and "letdown" which, in itself, is also an almost indescribable pleasure.

For the female member of the marriage team, the situation is a little different. Just inside the opening of the vulva is a small organ called the clitoris, made of tissue similar to that of the glans penis. It is usually very sensitive, and when stimulated during intercourse or manually, causes a tension and sexual readiness comparable to that in the male. In addition, other areas of the vulva also are similarly sensitive and responsive to friction. When these parts are stimulated, a lubricating fluid is produced that makes the insertion of the erect male penis easier. For the female, however, sexual stimulation is a great deal more complex than it is for the male.

Once sexually stimulated, a female may experience the tension, the "explosion," and the sudden release and relaxation that a male experiences in orgasm. Female orgasm is not, however, accompanied by any discharge of fluid, and the orgasm is not in any way connected with becoming pregnant. Moreover, although female orgasm produces pleasure comparable to that of male orgasm, it is not always a requirement for sexual satisfaction or for pleasure in sexual intercourse. Misunderstanding of this fact is the cause of a good deal of the difficulty in sexual adjustment commonly assumed to be one of the major factors in successful marriage.

The whole subject of sexual interaction in marriage can be summed up rather briefly by considering the relative importance attached to orgasm by men and women. For men orgasm is usually involved in sexual intercourse, whatever the purpose.

Most men in our culture, whether or not they are concerned with the equality of sexes in the right to enjoy the pleasures of sexual intercourse, feel that unless the wife responds in sexual intercourse in a way that indicates she also finds it pleasurable, it is *he* rather than his wife who has failed somehow. This is a difficult idea for women to understand, perhaps, but it is nonetheless a very important factor in sexual interaction. Almost all that is written about "techniques" contributes to this attitude.

The wife's sexual satisfaction is not necessarily measured in terms of orgasm. Studies have shown that countless wives who regard their sexual relationships as highly gratifying and satisfactory have never experienced orgasm at all—or haven't recognized it as such. Women have an extremely varied understanding of what orgasm is and may attach less importance to it than men do. The point is simply that a wife's feeling of satisfaction in sexual interaction frequently is enough, whether or not orgasm is involved.

Today it is theoretically possible that the attitudes of both men and women toward sex, in and out of marriage, are different from those held in the past. But there is no scientific evidence that they differ basically, despite the new sexual freedom. In any case, the matter of orgasm itself is pretty definitely fixed biologically. Advances in contraception may possibly have changed the psychological pattern somewhat, but apparently not in a very fundamental way.

Anything approaching satisfactory sexual interaction in marriage requires that both partners understand the differences in the ways immediate sexual desires are aroused in the male and female. For the wife, this is particularly important, because her own general sexual desires may be less pressing and less frequent than those of her husband. For the husband this understanding is important because his pleasure and satisfaction in sexual intercourse is certainly increased by a feeling that his wife shares, at least to some extent, his interest and desire at a specific time.

One writer summed up the differences in male and female sexual arousal with this statement: "Men are erotic—women are romantic."

Male sexual arousal is not entirely dependent upon external stimuli; males also have physical sexual needs produced by internal factors. The accumulation of seminal fluid sometimes reaches the point where the pressure, mainly physical in nature, has to be released. This accounts for the spontaneous and involuntary phenomenon of "nocturnal emissions." The pressure of seminal fluid has an erotic effect in itself, and for this reason male sexual arousal can be as much due to internal physiological processes as to external stimuli. This fact is frequently disregarded when sexual intercourse is idealized as an expression of love. Females do not experience physical need in the same way.

Apart from this, male sexual desires may be stimulated by a variety of causes that females often do not understand. Simple nervous tension may be, for the male, a sexual stimulus. For instance, some airplane pilots in World War II reported involuntary erection and ejaculation during their first solo flights. The same sexual excitement and stimulation was reported in connection with combat.

Aside from the erotic results of tension, males are more likely than females to be stimulated by sexual fantasies about the other sex, by portrayals of sexual activity in literature or the theater. Nude photographs, erotic stories, and simply viewing the opposite sex are causes of sexual arousal in males. Short skirts and more or less unconscious display of sexually associated physical attributes by women may cause intense sexual arousal for males—a fact that females sometimes use for their own purposes, consciously or unconsciously.

Whereas male sexual arousal is frequently, or usually, almost instantaneous, female sexual arousal is usually slow and gradual and depends more upon circumstances than upon immediate and obvious stimuli. Love stories in movies, on television, or in books are much more potent forces in sexual arousal for females than they are for males. These are not usually the kind of stories described as "pornographic." They are simply romantic stories, which males may enjoy without being sexually aroused.

Under appropriate romantic circumstances, females are also sexually aroused by physical contact in the areas of the body called *erogenous zones*. These include the breasts and the clitoris—but may, for individuals, be associated with many other areas of the body. The essential point is that sexual arousal for the female is a slow process, whereas for the male it is comparatively quick.

Because of the basic differences in the way male and female sexual desires are stimulated, communication about sexual interaction is vital to both marriage partners. Sexual intercourse is, in itself, a form of communication in which each separate experience may have its own special and individual message. But communication about sexual interaction is probably the most important and at the same time certainly one of the most difficult aspects of sex in marriage.

Whether you are a husband or a wife, how do you say to your

partner, "I want to have sexual intercourse"? And how do you reply, "So do I"? Or, "All right, I'm not very enthusiastic about it; but I'll go along"? Or, "I'm sorry, but I just don't want to have intercourse now"? Equally important are the messages exchanged during intercourse itself and in the preliminary activities leading to intercourse. Most couples develop their own sign language and codes for sexual communication. One woman, interviewed in a study of this subject, reported she always knew when her husband was going to want intercourse by the fact that he kicked the cat out of the way when he came home from work on those evenings.

Sign language is good, but so are words. There is no reason at all why a good marriage team should not be able to communicate in words about their sexual desires and responses. Although verbal communication about sexual interaction is not for many people part of sexual intercourse itself, a great many difficulties in sexual adjustment could certainly be avoided or solved if husband and wife could learn to talk frankly and openly about sexual interaction at times when sexual arousal is not an immediate factor. The wife should be able to identify, verbally, her erogenous zones and to discuss openly and frankly with her husband her sexual feelings. And a husband should be able to express his desires and responses openly and verbally.

Lack of verbal communication about sexual interaction, both between husband and wife and in society in general, has led to a great many myths, mistaken notions, and unanswered questions about sex. The remainder of this chapter will take up some of these briefly and concisely.

FREQUENCY OF INTERCOURSE. Frequency of intercourse depends on a number of factors, like the age of the marriage partners, the length of time they have been married, and personality characteristics. It is probably safe to say, however, that most young married couples have sexual intercourse about two or three times a week. There is nothing wrong with a higher or lower frequency. Everything depends upon the wishes and desires of the married couple.

MENSTRUATION AND INTERCOURSE. Most authorities agree that there is no medical or physiological reason for avoiding intercourse during menstruation. Of course, there are individual and psychological considerations, and these probably influence the responsiveness of both partners. But there is nothing "wrong" or "dangerous" about intercourse while menstruation is occurring.

POSITIONS IN INTERCOURSE. There are no magic positions for intercourse, although some of the marriage manuals suggest there may be. Whatever is most comfortable and pleasing to both marriage partners is the best. Positions in intercourse, however, tend to become habitual, and there is unquestionably value in experimenting with different positions.

TIME FOR SEXUAL INTERCOURSE. For some strange reason, our culture seems to suggest that sexual intercourse should take place only at night. The only possible reason for this restriction is that it may offer the greatest opportunity for privacy and freedom from interruption. There is nothing at all sacred about the night or evening hours as the only proper time for sexual intercourse.

NUDITY. There is no doubt that nudity provides greater satisfaction and freedom in sexual intercourse than partial nudity, although there are class differences and individual preferences in this practice. Some women have reported that nudity was more an obstacle to sexual adjustment than any other factor. The pleasures of sexual intercourse at least call for the complete accessibility of all parts of the body for both partners.

SIZE OF GENITALS. One of the persistent and pernicious myths about sex and sexual intercourse is that the length and size of the male penis and the size of the female vagina influence sexual adjustment. Except for a few rare instances involving extreme differences in size, it is definitely untrue. There is no relationship between the size of the genitals of either male or female and the ability to provide or achieve sexual pleasure and satisfaction.

APHRODISIACS. Another myth connected with sexual interaction is that there are foods and drugs or ointments, called aphrodisiacs, that induce sexual desire. In fact, such things do not exist. Some drugs, including alcohol, may tend to lower inhibitions regarding sex, but they do not directly stimulate sexual desire.

PREMATURE EJACULATION. It is not uncommon, especially in the early period of marriage, for the male to reach a sexual climax almost before his wife has begun to experience sexual stimulation. This may be embarrassing to him and frustrating to his wife. Sometimes the problem may call for medical advice, but it can usually be corrected by learning how to control the pre-intercourse activities. Decreasing the sensitivity of the glans penis by the use of a condom (not for contraceptive purposes) or by the use of certain desensitizing salves or jellies is a possibility. The cause of premature ejaculation, however, is usually more psychological than physical. For most men, the important thing is knowing that the phenomenon is by no means unique to them and that it does not indicate a personal weakness or lack of adequate masculinity.

IMPOTENCY. Along with premature ejaculation, there is another occasional problem called impotency—the inability to have a satisfactory penis erection or to achieve ejaculation. Impotency has nothing to do with sterility, which is the inability of the male to fertilize the female's ovum and may be caused by any number of biological or physical situations. Almost always the cause of impotency is psychological except possibly in old age, and even then may be psychological. Only a long continued and persistent condition of impotency is cause for concern.

Clinical studies have shown that some impotence is caused by early sexual experience and conditioning. There are cases on record indicating that some men who are relatively impotent with their wives are very potent with other women. Sometimes this may be due to the wife's lack of sexual responsiveness. Sometimes it may be because of psychological idealization of his wife. He may be potent with a prostitute, but not with his wife.

Sometimes temporary impotency may be caused by worry, fear, or other problems having nothing to do with the marriage itself. And sometimes it may be caused by a sort of disillusionment, resulting from the failure of the partners to work together as a team in areas not involving sex directly. In any event, if this area of sex and marriage presents a problem that persists, the services of a qualified psychological marriage counselor are required.

FRIGIDITY. The female counterpart to male impotency is called frigidity. This simply means that she does not respond to sexual interaction at all. The causes of frigidity are likely to be much the same as for male impotency; but the condition occurs more frequently among females than chronic impotency among males. Furthermore, it is sometimes more deep-seated and more difficult to correct. Girls are apt to be somewhat more "afraid of sex" than boys, usually because of their upbringing. Traditionally, at least, girls are more protected than boys, and one way protection is implemented is by making them fear sex. Today this practice is not as common as it once was, but it still is a factor where frigidity is a problem. Frigidity should not be confused with temporary lack of interest in sexual activity, which can be caused by much the same factors that produce temporary impotency.

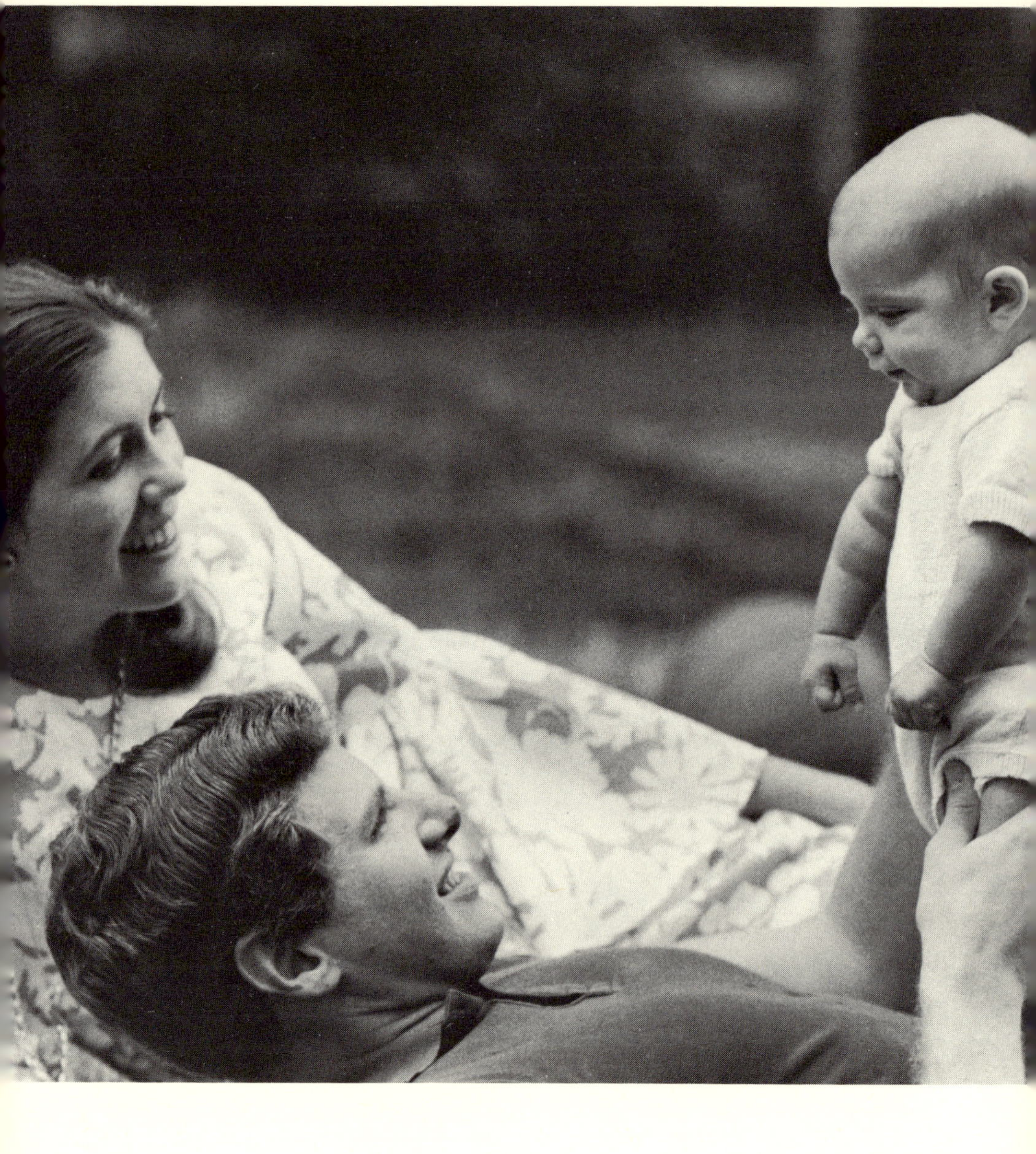

12

Planning for Parenthood

> Families, when a child is born,
> Want it to be intelligent.
> I, through intelligence—
> Having wrecked my whole life,
> Only hope the baby will prove
> Ignorant and stupid.
> Then he will crown a tranquil life
> By becoming a Cabinet Minister.
>
> —Translated from the Chinese of
> Su Tung-p'o (1036–1101) by ARTHUR WALEY

The title of this chapter should convey two different but related ideas. One is that of "planned parenthood," meaning that through the use of contraceptive devices and methods the marriage team may make decisions about when to have their first child, how many children to have and how spaced, or whether or not to have children at all. The other idea is that, whether or not planned parenthood is involved, parents must plan ahead for children from the time pregnancy is recognized. Children profoundly affect marriage and the interpersonal relationships of the married partners, and there are many questions and problems associated with parenthood, either planned or unplanned, which are both interesting and important. Although this chapter will look ahead to parenthood, regardless of the circumstances that bring it about, it is necessary first to point out a few facts and misunderstandings about contraception that may not be well known.

Aside from complete avoidance of sexual intercourse, there is no method of contraception that is entirely effective. That is why it is best not to delineate completely all the possible methods. Today contraceptive pills, diaphragms, condoms, and the so-called rhythm method are most frequently used. But any method that involves the use of a chemical should be carefully checked with a qualified physician before attempted. If, for any reason, this is impractical, advice should be sought from the Planned Parenthood Association of America. Most large towns and cities have offices and clinics, which can be located from the telephone book, and one may write to the headquarters of the association, the Planned Parenthood Federation of America, Inc., 515 Madison Avenue, New York, N.Y. 10022.

Among the methods of contraception, one deserves special attention here. Determining what period in the menstrual cycle sexual intercourse is least likely to result in pregnancy is definitely not a "do it yourself" project. If the rhythm or "safe period" method is to be used in birth control, its effectiveness depends upon professional record-keeping over a long period of time in order to determine even approximately the menstrual rhythm. Once this is determined, the general rule is that pregnancy is most likely to result from intercourse approximately two weeks before menstruation begins. It does not necessarily indicate when pregnancy is *least* likely to occur.

The rhythm method is the only one approved by some religions, but it is probably the least effective and sure of all methods, even when competent medical advice is sought. The menstrual cycle is not absolutely regular, for one thing. And adherence to mathematically based schedules for intercourse is, to say the least, difficult and possibly psychologically damaging.

There is much yet to be learned about the possible effects of contraceptive pills, so it is possible that some of the weird ideas you may hear expressed have just a little validity. For instance, there is some evidence that twins are a bit more likely to result from intercourse after use of the pill is discontinued. This is, however, still only a guess, not an established fact. There are increasing evidences that certain harmful effects for the mother or for the child may be associated with prior use of the contraceptive pill. The medical profession is still watching and experimenting, and in the meantime thousands upon thousands of women are using the pill without apparent bad effects. However, there is a chance that widespread use may result in defects through successive generations. Moreover, the pill itself is not 100-percent effective, just as the mechanical devices are not 100-percent effective. Perhaps the combination of diaphragm and contraceptive jelly, which was standard before the pill was invented, is still the safest and most effective method, but there are certain aesthetic considerations involved here which make it for many people less attractive than the simple process of taking a pill.

There are, however, some ideas about contraception that are definitely myths. One is that the prolonged use of any device or method ultimately affects the ability to conceive, or that it decreases the sexual satisfactions of either or both husband and wife. Some folklore attaches even more dire results to the use of contraceptives. The truth is that if husband and wife agree on the method of contraception and if the chosen method is based on good professional advice from a doctor, it has no effect other than to allow them to have children more or less when they want them. Under normal and satisfactory circumstances, use of contraceptives is more likely to increase rather than decrease sexual pleasure.

Along with mistaken ideas about the effect of contraceptive measures goes another sexual myth, which certainly needs to be corrected. This is the idea that a woman cannot conceive another child while she is nursing a previous one. This belief appears to be well established for many people, but it is completely false. Pregnancy results at any time a sperm enters an egg cell, and egg cells are produced and are carried along the Fallopian tubes at more or less regular intervals when a woman is not pregnant.

Assuming that the marriage team has made a decision, agreeable and satisfactory to both members, concerning family planning, the next decision is when to have the first child. Of course, the time cannot be set precisely. The date the child is conceived and finally born will be determined by many, many factors. The basic decision is when to stop contraception procedures.

Among marriage counselors and others who have studied the effect of children upon husband-wife relationships, there is some disagreement about the most desirable time for the first child. Most books on marriage suggest that, where planned parenthood is involved, the married couple should plan to have their first-born child some time after at least a year of adjustment, learning to live together as husband and wife.

Some students of marriage have rejected this theory and have found that there are very good reasons for the early arrival of the first child. In fact, it is sometimes said that an early first child actually helps the couple become a team, but only from a psychological and an emotional point of view.

One study of what wives considered the best time for having the first child, looking back on their own experience, found that 87 percent thought that the best timing was 24 to 29 months after marriage. The same study showed that 55 percent of them thought that under 8 months was too soon and 38 percent thought that 8 to 11 months was too soon. This study, however, revealed that the reasons given for the first child's being "too soon" or "just right" placed less importance on the marital adjustment aspect than on the financial aspect of the timing. Although 76 percent of the wives felt that under eight months was too soon for financial reasons, only 37 percent found marriage adustment a factor. And 52 percent found that under eight months was undesirable because it kept them from "enjoying things." However cold-blooded it may sound, putting off the birth of the first child for a year or so seems to be justified on financial grounds, even if not on adjustment or emotional grounds.

Many people seem to regard about one year between the first and second child as the most desirable spacing interval. The reasons usually given emphasize the importance of a playmate for both children and the relative ease of child-care for children of approximately the same age. Almost as many people regard 19 to 24 months as the best interval, and even more people consider that this interval makes child-care easier. The individual decision probably depends chiefly on the kind of experience parents have with the first child.

Assuming that genuine planned parenthood is practiced and that there is no failure of contraceptive measures, planning ahead as to how many children to have involves a great many different factors. Most people hope to have at least two children and usually not more than four. In general, the number of children actually desired after marriage is considerably less than the number people say they would like to have before they are married. Financial considerations are very likely one reason for this change of mind. Also, the first child brings home to most people for the first time the full understanding of the problems, difficulties, and disruptions of married life which children unquestionably cause, and the tasks associated with some twenty years of responsibility for child-rearing.

Sometimes a couple has more children than they had originally planned on for a curious cultural reason. Apparently Americans value highly the idea of "a boy for me, a girl for you," with the result that when the first and second children are of the same sex, a great many parents want a third or fourth child on the gamble that it will be of the opposite sex. Along with this goes the fact that most people believe the family should include at least one boy, since only through a son can the family name be passed on. It is difficult to insure this situation because, although there are approximately 106 boys born for every 100 girls, the sex of children is always a gamble. Until recently, scientists thought sex determination in planning a family was impossible, since the pairings of the chromosomes that determines sex could not be controlled. For all usual circumstances this is still true, but a great many experiments have been carried out in very recent years and there is some reason to believe that eventually it will be possible for parents to have a girl or a boy by choice.

In planning for three or more, it is obvious that finances must be carefully considered. Some people don't like to think about parenthood and finances, on the ground that it detracts from the full appreciation and joys of parenthood. The financial implications of parenthood may be sobering, but a little realism is a good thing in the long run. If you are going to plan when to have children or plan for them, it is a good idea to compare their probable cost with the state of your bank account and estimated future income.

The total cost of the first child from the time of conception to the time it is born will usually be at least $700. This includes medical expenses, hospital, "infant goods," and other normal expenses. Somebody has to pay this cost, and it does not make much difference whether the money comes from insurance, gifts from other people, or other sources. Somebody has to pay—and in the long run it will be you and your spouse.

This average figure is based on the assumption that there are no complications in the birth, and it depends, too, on such things as total income. Statistics show that people in the income bracket of about $6,000 to $7,000 spend 10 percent of their annual income for the cost of the first child, whereas people with an annual income above $12,000 spend around 11 percent for the first child.

The initial expenses of having a child are only the beginning. The U.S. Department of Agriculture and the Department of Labor figure that on the basis of costs in 1969, the total expenditure for raising one child from birth to age eighteen runs from $20,750 to $34,200. Although there may be some bit of truth in the theory that children are "cheaper by the dozen," because the cost of shelter is more widely distributed and the cost of clothing can be reduced through "hand-me-downs," the total cost of raising a number of children to the age of eighteen is rather staggering. Four children, aged eighteen to twenty-five, could have cost about $100,000.

All planning involves recognition of possibilities and probabilities, along with emotional preparation for meeting whatever happens. Regardless of planning, the first child is a crisis in marriage. By this we mean that the arrival of the first child will cause a very definite change in life, for which past experience almost certainly has not provided. One sociologist has made a very interesting study of this subject entitled "Parenthood as Crisis." Apart from his statistical findings, his report of the verbal expressions of first-time parents is revealing, and sums up the considerations you can think about in planning for or anticipating the first stages of becoming parents.

> *The mothers reported the following feelings or experiences in adjusting to the first child: loss of sleep (especially during the early months); chronic "tiredness" or exhaustion; extensive confinement to the home and the resulting curtailment of their social contacts; giving up the satisfactions and the income of outside employment; additional washing and ironing; guilt at not being a "better" mother; the long hours and seven days (and nights) a week necessary in caring for an infant; decline in their housekeeping standards; and worry about their appearance (increased weight after pregnancy, etc.).*
>
> *The fathers echoed most of the above adjustments but also added a few of their own: decline in sexual response of wife; economic pressure resulting from wife's retirement plus additional expenditures necessary for child; interference with social life; worry about a second pregnancy in the near future; and a general disenchantment with the parental role.*[19]

Becoming parents is probably the most severe test of marriage teamwork you will ever face. It is not only a matter of dividing up the jobs that have to be done or taking turns at changing diapers and washing them—something that husbands notoriously dislike. It is a great deal more than this in several ways that need to be faced very frankly and bluntly.

In the first place, there are two possibly conflicting values at stake. One of these is the future of the child, in terms not only of his healthy physical development but, sometimes even more important, his healthy personality development. Children, from infancy on, are like sponges, soaking up the feelings and attitudes of those with whom they live. They have to be socialized—that is, they must learn how to get along with other people and with society at large. This is an essential part of development and education. One crisis of parenthood arises from the necessity of presenting to the child the kind of relationships that he can emulate, meanwhile avoiding the outward display of conflicts and strains or obsessions that will indicate subconsciously to the child that this is the way adults are. If the father and mother differ in their ideas and expressions of ideas with respect to child-rearing, the child may become confused.

The other value is the marriage itself—both its quality and its duration. In the study of parenthood and crisis referred to above, the researchers found no significant difference between the crisis-producing power of "wanted" and "unwanted" children. The searchers didn't clarify their definition of "unwanted," but it is reasonable to assume that they were thinking of unexpected and unanticipated children, and that they assumed that the unexpectedness or the lack of positive wanting was shared fairly equally by husband and wife.

If one parent had wanted the child and the other had definitely not wanted the child, the effects of the parenthood crisis could be enormously amplified. It is probably generally true that wives are more likely to want to become mothers than husbands are to become fathers, and this is precisely the reason why the marriage team needs to reach an agreement about either deliberately seeking to produce a child or accepting the results of their sexual intercourse.

It is not difficult for a wife to allow herself deliberately to become pregnant. It may be a misguided effort to "hold" the husband when the marriage becomes shaky. Neither the marriage nor the child is likely to benefit by this sort of maneuver. The husband is almost certain to resent the child and consequently be less successful as a father. He will also resent his wife's action and distrust her. This crisis of parenthood could become the disaster that wrecks the marriage.

Quite apart from either crisis or disaster, there are some other facts of life that need to be considered in planning for parenthood. The old adage, "Three is a crowd," is true in marriage just as in social life. With the first child, the old role pattern-structure of the marriage is completely changed. Instead of only two people interacting, there are now three; that means six separate interrelationships. The roles are possibly conflicting or awkward until they have been learned and adjustments made.

For a great many young parents living in small apartments, three is very literally a crowd. If, like many married couples, you have an apartment with a good-sized living room, a kitchenette, a bath, and a small bedroom, you must face the problem of where the baby is going to sleep. If he has his crib in the bedroom along with your bed, when you get up to change his diapers or feed him, the activity will disturb both of you. Whatever happens is likely to interrupt the sleep of the other partner as well. Furthermore, babies do a lot more crying than non-parents realize. Sometimes they cry because they have colic and sometimes they cry simply because they are so healthy they have to express themselves vocally.

Suppose you decide that the living room is, after all, the best place for the baby's crib. In some ways this may work out very well at first. The living room, however, is going to become an extremely untidy place unless you and your partner are better housekeepers than most people. This crib arrangement can also make the living room exceptionally crowded and difficult to move around in, and will restrict the use of the room for entertaining, especially at night.

Then there are some other effects of the small or restricted living quarters. Unless you are unusually well off, you can't afford a babysitter very frequently. This means that you are going to be pretty generally "restricted to quarters," and you are going to feel the need for some sort of social contacts outside the nuclear family. When you invite friends in for an evening, you put the baby in your bed. But the friends may be noisy, and even if they are not, there are four adults talking. The bedroom isn't far enough away to muffle the noise, so baby is awake and crying. The next time you invite the friends they may find themselves busy. You can go on through a long list of the disadvantages of crowded living, even when the baby is very small.

By the time he is a year old, the earlier stages will appear blissful by comparison. Keep these few facts in mind while you paint your own picture of what could happen: (1) Young children, despite popular superstition, do *not* sleep twenty hours a day. (2) Within an incredibly short time babies discover ways of locomotion you wouldn't believe possible. They can be under foot long before they are able to walk. (3) No matter how much your friends like children in general, when they come to see you they want to visit with you—not the baby.

A good deal of this discussion may seem like arguments for not having any children at all. This is definitely not the case. These points are made to encourage wise and practical decisions about when to have children and how many to have.

Most marriage teams want, and expect, to have children. If for any reason they do not produce them themselves, they may adopt them. The basic principles of parenthood are the same. One further consideration, however, must be taken into account whether or not children are planned, expected, or adopted. This factor is heredity.

Understanding heredity is important in planning for parenthood, because misunderstandings and worries about some facts of heredity can influence not only the family planning but also the marriage relationship after the birth of the child.

The science of heredity and genetics is covered in detail in other books, but some general facts should be taken into account in planning for parenthood. If there is any known history in the families of either husband or wife of hereditary illness, or if you have any suspicion at all that there may be some hereditary factor that could affect your children adversely, it would be a good idea to check with an expert before making final plans for parenthood. The chances are that his report will be reassuring rather than the other way around, and at least you will know what the odds are. Doctors can usually give some help in this respect. Also, "heredity counseling clinics" are springing up all over the United States. These clinics are often connected with medical centers or universities, and counseling is done by geneticists trained in the science of human heredity. Usually their services are free. If there is any reason whatsoever to question whether your baby will be normal, and if you are anywhere in the vicinity of one of these clinics, it is certainly worth checking to see what can be learned.

The most generally feared aspect of heredity has to do with the Rh factor of the blood. Here your doctor is fully competent to give advice; but in planning ahead it is a good idea to have a blood test and get the advice before rather than after pregnancy. Adoption agencies usually cover these areas of heredity pretty thoroughly before permitting adoption.

There remains one more aspect of planning ahead which, if you are like most other people, you won't think much about until you actually become parents, although if you are really operating as a marriage team you should give a good deal of thought to it ahead of time. This consideration has to do with how you are going to bring up your children after you have them.

Naturally, you cannot plan every little detail of how you are going to bring up your children. It is, nevertheless, very definitely a good idea for the marriage team, using the regular team process of study, discussion, and compromise, to decide on certain broad principles of child-rearing. Lack of parental agreement on some of these broad principles can do a great deal of damage to the personality of the child as he grows up. No definite rules or information can be offered in this area because everything depends on the individual parents. They should, however, reach agreement and follow a general plan based on agreement in connection with the following areas of child-rearing.

RATING OF CHILD BEHAVIOR VALUES. Do you agree that children should be seen and not heard? How do you rate the values of obedience, neatness and cleanliness, respect for parents, and other qualities of child behavior?

DISCIPLINE. Whose job will it be to administer what kinds of discipline? Are there any forms of discipline either member of the marriage team feels should never be used? If so, how does the other marriage partner feel about it? Perhaps an especially important consideration here is the possibility that the wife may feel virtually all discipline is the job of the father. This doesn't work very well, because it usually delays the discipline and is much less effective. At the same time it creates a father-image that can be very damaging to later father-child relationships.

SPOILING THE CHILD. Are you going to have any general rules about giving in to the demands of your young children? It is a pretty good idea to get this sort of thing settled very early because it is the basis for some easily acquired and expensive habits, both financial and emotional. Some mothers have the habit of buying some little toy or "goodie" for their toddlers every time they go to the grocery store, and some parents have actually said that children are no fun unless they are spoiled. Do you think you and your partner will be in agreement on this point after you have children? Truthfully, there is more involved in this aspect of child-rearing than appears at first. An overindulgent parent is never a good one, but sometimes, and under some circumstances, a *reasonably* indulgent father and a *reasonably* strict mother (or vice versa) make a good combination for the benefit of the child.

RELIGION. What are your ideas about the religious training of children? This does not include the problems of religious training created by interfaith marriage. The point here is whether or not you are going to teach your child to say bedtime prayers or take him to Sunday School, and how you are going to explain concepts like God and Heaven. The importance of this kind of policy decision depends on your own attitude toward religion as a married couple. If you are both religious, the situation may be taken care of. But a great many parents who are not themselves religious may have a feeling that their children, nonetheless, should be exposed to religion. Do you and your partner agree in this whole area?

These are some of the subjects you can profitably discuss in planning for parenthood. They are very realistic considerations. Along with them goes a different kind of practical decision, one that is seldom discussed and one which social scientists apparently have not investigated. It is how you are going to name your children.

A favorite pastime of practically all parents-to-be is discussing names for the forthcoming offspring. There is a good deal of significance in this part of planning for parenthood. The selection of names may possibly reveal a good deal about husband-wife relationships. It may also affect the extended family relationships.

Although there is no data on the subject, naming a child after one of its grandparents is done, more likely than not, to please the grandparent and just possibly to have some effect on in-law relationships. At the same time, however, it might perhaps suggest a preference for one set of grandparents over the other, thereby creating a problem. On the whole, though, a name that will help to give the child a sense of identity and of belonging to a kinship group or some definite social network is better than a name which has no significance at all. Naming, therefore, should not be for the benefit of the person from whom the name is borrowed so much as for the benefit of the child.

Another method of name selection is to choose a name carried by a prominent actor or actress or other celebrity. One difficulty with this method is that the child may be saddled with a first name shared by a high percentage of other children of the same age. This can cause considerable confusion, as every elementary-school teacher knows. Girl's names, especially, seem to come in fashion cycles. Sometimes you can make a pretty good guess at the age of a woman by her name.

In any method of name selection, one important consideration should be remembered. Some names almost automatically are shortened to nicknames, at least by the child's peer group. In selecting a name, therefore, you may also be selecting a nickname, and you might as well decide right from the beginning whether you like the nickname as well as the given name. You can't call a son "William" and refuse to let his playmates call him "Bill." And don't choose "Margaret" if you really have an aversion to "Maggie."

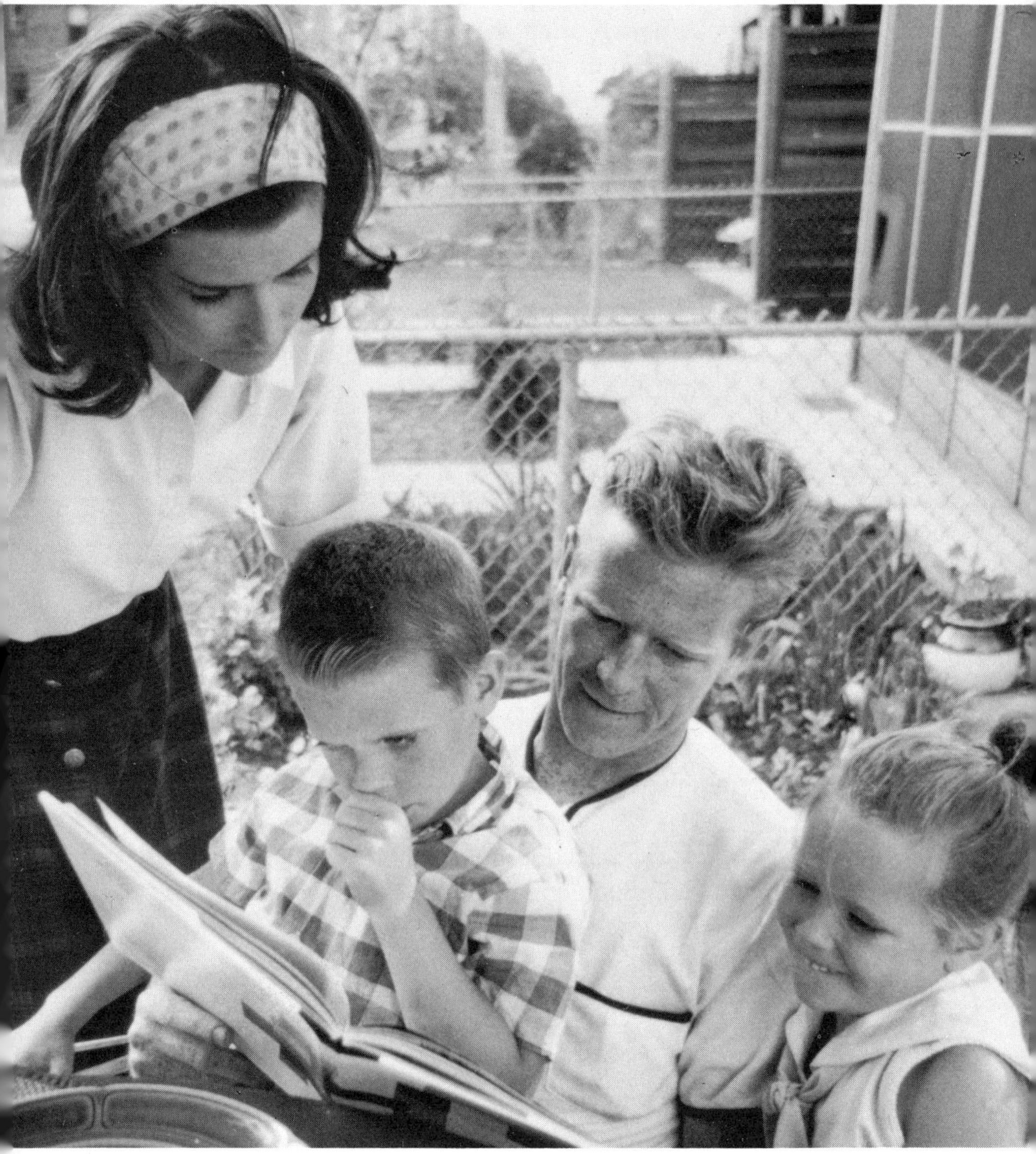

13

Values

> It asks a little of us here.
> It asks of us a certain height.
> So when at times the mob is swayed
> To carry praise or blame too far,
> We may take something like a star
> To stay our minds on and be staid.
> —ROBERT FROST, "Take Something Like a Star"

A value is the relative worth, desirability, or importance of a thing, a way of acting, or any aspect of life in comparison with other things and modes of behavior.

The foundation of a value is its contribution to human existence, basic needs, and reasonably happy and comfortable living. People do not all have the same requirements for existence, the same psychological and material needs, so values are different according to circumstances. For an extreme illustration, an electric deep-freezer is valuable in the United States, but has little or no value in the Arctic. The pattern also applies to behavior. For instance, where getting food requires hard work and special tools, and involves money as a medium of exchange, honesty about money is a value. Where living is easy, as in the South Pacific, where much food is available for the taking, honesty about money is not always in itself a value.

Values can differ according to circumstances as well. When household cleanliness is important to health, cleanliness has value, but this is not always the case, as with nomadic people who move from place to place frequently. The value of wifely obedience to the husband based on economic necessity is important in some cultures, but less so in others.

The practical, material bases for values usually change with time and become represented by customs, laws, and normative roles. The values they reflect are usually abstract; they aren't directly associated with things so much as with ideas. Among important American values are freedom of the individual, independence, and democracy. We have customs, laws, and normative roles calculated to preserve these values. In cultures that don't attach as much, or any, importance to these abstracts, the way of life is different from ours because it isn't organized around the same values.

Basic values create other values. The basic value of individual freedom has resulted in the value of equality of the sexes. This has led to the value of individual choice of a marriage partner. The marriage team idea is based on the value of individual freedom along with all the resulting and associated values, including independence and democracy. This complex of interrelated values is called a *value system*, which is made up of a number of values, each with its own set of satellite values. Sometimes certain values conflict with others, producing value conflicts that are similar to role conflicts. Moreover, values and value systems vary not only among major cultures, but among subcultures and socio-economic classes.

Individuals also attach varying degrees of importance to some of the basic cultural values. This, of course, is partly the result of subcultural influence, but it is also the result of individual emotional or material needs. Poverty, for instance, makes survival a much more significant value than freedom or democracy or independence. A well-heeled but emotionally insecure person, however, may value prestige or power above all else, and base his entire value system on this value.

VALUES

Individual values and value systems affect marriage in many direct and uncomplicated ways, which are nonetheless packed with emotional TNT that can be exploded by a spark, but they can be used to promote the happiness and satisfaction of the marriage team, depending on how well the partners work together as a team.

Brief analysis of a few studies will show how individual values and value systems are reflected in everyday habits and routines.

> Mr. A attaches a great deal of importance to getting up early in the morning. He explains that this is the way he was brought up; so he gets out of bed every morning at five-thirty and starts puttering around with whatever chores have to be done. Mrs. A likes to stay in bed as late as possible.

For Mr. A, getting up early is not a value, however desirable it appears to him, but conformity to the pattern of his upbringing is a value. Doing household chores in the early morning probably is a reflection of the same value. Mrs. A's staying in bed doesn't necessarily reflect an individual value system at all. There is nothing critical for the marriage in this situation unless Mr. A feels that his personal value system should apply to Mrs. A.

> Neatness and good housekeeping are the ruling passions in Mrs. B's life. She regards a dirty ashtray or an unwashed dish as an evidence of sin. She objects to Mr. B's smoking, not because of the health hazard, but because it makes for an untidy living room.

It is clear that prestige is one of Mrs. B's individual values. She assigns the value to the feeling of superiority over other housewives who aren't as neat as she is.

> Mrs. C believes that proper diet for her husband and children is of the utmost importance. Almost unconsciously she believes that all problems or possible problems in life are solved by "good eating habits." She insists that the children eat everything that is set before

them, and she makes sure that what they have is correctly balanced with respect to all dietary requirements. Mr. C is not as convinced as Mrs. C of the value of diet; but he goes along with her ideas because he believes that agreement of parents about matters of this sort is important—is a value.

Mr. and Mrs. C share at least one individual value system built on adherence to rules. In this instance the rules are laid down by certain writers about diet and by others on child-rearing. If they had read further or read other books, they would have learned that their pattern is not approved by all "authorities" and is, in fact, disapproved of by most in some respects. But this discovery probably would not have changed their pattern. They feel the need for guidance in child-rearing and so they value conformity to standards. The set of standards they value is probably dictated by which set they are first exposed to. The value expressed here is not in the standards—the rigid diet and agreement of parents. For Mrs. C, the value is conformity; for Mr. C, the avoidance of disagreement.

There are other aspects of values not covered by the illustrations above. If a young man who earns $50.00 a week buys a $3,000 automobile with "nothing down and low monthly payments" (for 48 months), one might say he has "no sense of values." Usually, this means simply that he is financially foolish, which he is. But, there are two other meanings in the phrase "sense of values."

One is that the young man doesn't have the ability to recognize a value when he sees one. He just isn't "value oriented." He never even thinks about values as a basis for decision. The other is that he can't discriminate wisely among the values he does perceive. For him, owning the car, even though he's "in hock" for it, is the overwhelming value. Just as some people have no "card sense" and seem unable to play any card game, there are unquestionably, people who never develop "value sense." For a successful marriage, however, a couple must make an earnest effort to do so by learning to weigh cultural values and individual values against a standard.

If the financially foolish young man was unmarried and had a

VALUES

sense of values, he might have weighed the value of the automobile in terms of pleasure, status, or whatever other value led him to want the car, against his personal financial security. But in marriage, all values are weighed against the standard of marriage itself.

Here are some of the American cultural values that must be weighed in the balance with marriage. Try arranging all these values in order of their importance in general—not in marriage—according to your own ideas or prejudices. Some may, possibly, have about equal importance in your eyes.

Individualism—dignity and worth of the individual
Love
Sex equality
Financial security
Freedom
Happiness
Family—in the sense of belonging (identification)
Conformity to the cultural norms
Status—in the sense of prestige

Now think specifically of some cultural values attached to marriage. How do you rank these values that are culturally regarded as implicit in marriage? Some of the general values are, naturally, included.

Security
Companionship
Happiness
Sexual gratification
Parenthood
Love
Status
Personal fulfillment (We leave this purposely undefined.)

Any decision and any policy of the marriage team involves weighing individual values, general cultural values, and marriage values against each other and balancing all of them with the success of the marriage itself.

There is no right or wrong order for ranking the values listed above. You are entitled to your own ideas, but when you and your marriage teammate differ greatly in the relative importance assigned to these values, teamwork is going to be especially important, and perhaps difficult. Part or all of the difficulty may result from another aspect of values, which, so far, has only been implied or hinted.

This element is false values—values assigned, individually or by the marriage team, to ideas and actions that conflict with cultural value systems for stated reasons other than those that in fact operate. For instance, the cultural value of independence and freedom may be used simply as an excuse for rebellion against parents or other authorities for hidden and unrecognized psychological reasons that have little or nothing to do with values.

More commonly perhaps, a false value may simply be unrealistic, as in the case of the young man who bought a car he couldn't afford. Usually, false values are assigned on the basis of a tradition, or custom, that no longer has significance in either the practical or economic areas of living. Frequently, these are associated with religion, use of leisure time, extended family relationships, authority, and many of the other aspects of marriage. A true value and value system is one that makes important those qualities of marriage and life that are not casually acquired. They must be reached for, worked for, and sacrificed for.

Sources

[1] Margaret Mead. *Male and Female.* New York, 1949.

[2] *Portland Oregonian,* April 26, 1967.

[3] Robert Varga. "Dilemmas of a Househusband," *Saturday Review,* Jan. 2, 1965.

[4] J. Richard Udry. *The Social Context of Marriage.* Philadelphia, 1966.

[5] "The Working Wife and Mother," *Changing Times: The Kiplinger Magazine,* July 1965.

[6] Mary Feeley for the Associated Press. Quoted in *Portland Oregonian,* May 1, 1967.

[7] Ernest W. Burgess and Paul Wallin. *Engagement and Marriage.* Philadelphia, 1953.

[8] Betty Friedan. *The Feminine Mystique.* New York, 1963.

[9] Robert F. Winch. *The Modern Family,* rev. edn. New York, 1963.

[10] J. Richard Udry. *The Social Context of Marriage.* Philadelphia, 1966.

[11] D. M. Schneider and G. C. Homans. "Kinship Terminology in the American Kinship System," *American Anthropologist,* Dec. 1955.

[12] Daniel A. Prescott. "Role of Love in Human Development," *Journal of Home Economics,* March 1952.

[13] Erich Fromm. *Man for Himself.* New York, 1947.

[14] W. J. Goode. "The Theoretical Importance of Love," *American Sociological Review,* Feb. 1959, p. 41.

[15] Harry Stack Sullivan. *Conceptions of Modern Psychiatry*. New York, 1953.

[16] R. O. Blood, Jr. *Marriage*. New York, 1962.

[17] Gael Greene. *Sex and the College Girl*. New York, 1963.

[18] Anthony Storr. *Sexual Deviation*. Baltimore, 1964.

[19] E. E. Lemasters. "Parenthood as Crisis," *Marriage and Family Living*, Nov. 1957.

PICTURE CREDITS

Harbrace Photo: pp. 14, 40, 50, 64, 110, 122, 134, 162; Susan Johns: pp. 24, 92; Erika Stone: p. 148; Jim Theologos: pp. 4, 80.